MY CORPSE INSIDE

CRUX
THE GEORGIA SERIES IN
LITERARY NONFICTION

MY CORPSE INSIDE

WES JAMISON

The University of Georgia Press ■ *Athens*

Published by the University of Georgia Press
Athens, Georgia 30602
www.ugapress.org

Set in Minion Pro
Printed and bound by Sheridan Books, Inc.
The paper in this book meets the guidelines for permanence and durability of the Committee on Production Guidelines for Book Longevity of the Council on Library Resources.

Most University of Georgia Press titles are available from popular e-book vendors.

Printed in the United States of America
29 28 27 26 25 P 5 4 3 2 1

Library of Congress Cataloging-in-Publication Data

Names: Jamison, Wes author
Title: My corpse inside / Wes Jamison.
Description: Athens : The University of Georgia Press, 2025. | Series: Crux: the Georgia series in literary nonfiction | Includes bibliographical references.
Identifiers: LCCN 2025013815 | ISBN 9780820374949 paperback | ISBN 9780820374956 epub | ISBN 9780820374963 pdf
Subjects: LCSH: Jamison, Wes | Authors, American—20th century—Biography | Online social networks—Psychological aspects | Internet—Psychological aspects | LCGFT: Autobiographies | Essays
Classification: LCC PS3610.A49 Z46 2025 | DDC 813/.54—dc23/eng/20250410
LC record available at https://lccn.loc.gov/2025013815

Would you like to meet a ghost.

The advent of one's own identity demands a law that mutilates.

—JULIA KRISTEVA

CONTENTS

ACKNOWLEDGMENTS

A portion of this essay appears in *After the Art* as "Violent, Dark Revolts of Being." My gratitude to the editor.

Much of this essay owes itself to Cinephile and Feminist Theories, Howard Brown's Violence Recovery Project, the Domestic Violence Legal Clinic in Chicago, Dr. John Laudun, my dissertation committee, and, of course, UGA Press. Many thanks to you all.

I am so very grateful that I have surrounded myself with people who made the essaying more manageable, the grappling with all this blood, semen, and shit and insult I didn't know I wanted to put to page.

I want to extend a special thanks to the following individuals:

Doc McLemore, for the guidance, inspiration, and mentorship you gave; your inexorable belief in essaying and in me. For your Piscean way of intuiting the importance of these words long before they were ever written.

Dr. Kightley, for your sincerity and trust. For helping me make the most of a bad situation and, equally, for reassuring me that being queer is always already being queer enough.

M, my partner, for respecting the uncomfortable process. For making the space and time for it. For giving me the time. For seeing me at my least flattering moments—all those times I told you to stop looking at me, and yet.

My siblings, for the movies, least of all.

And my mother: This work could not have existed without you. Neither could I.

MY CORPSE INSIDE

Phone calls with my mother last for hours, and they always end on TV shows and movies we've watched since we spoke last. We need it, after talking about, usually, death and the news—but only that kind of news that we think is worth comment, the kind of news that predicts the end of humanity, which is, anymore, most kinds of news. She always starts with something new on or new to Netflix, and it's almost always something I haven't yet seen. *It's weird. You'll like it*, she says, although it's unclear exactly what she thinks I like. *Weird* designates something discomfiting and includes unlikely premises, complex cinematography, and a seemingly recent brand of quirky drama, the kind I always attribute to hipsters. I almost never watch them.

My suggestions are always few because they are usually horror, especially psychological horrors that she wouldn't or couldn't empathize with. Once, I convinced her to watch Darren Aronofsky's *Mother!* with me. As I physically recoiled from the sounds of the cult tearing apart a baby, a living baby, no longer living, she looked at me, watched my disgust, and said, *Oh, it's* just *a movie.* But in the past week, I've watched only one film, multiple times, one I had seen multiple times before that. I tell her it's for this project, which we also usually talk about.

She seems to listen intently, that unmuted silence from the phone, as I stutter to develop the language with her. I'm confronting the difficulty. It's all abstruse rhetorical gymnastics: Let's look at forty-year-old critical theory to find answers to impractical questions that no one, especially my mother, wants to ask, like *what is my body to me*, and *are we* inside *our bodies or* are *we them. To what does* I *refer*, and *if not* me, *then what.* I try to anchor myself to the psychology and psychoanalysis she picked up during her years spent working in mental health, I try to buoy myself with that. *Okay, you know the whole kill-your-father-have-sex-with-your-mother thing. Well, it's like that, but instead all we do is turn away from the nipple while being nursed, that's what Kristeva said.* It's a name she knows by now, Julia Kristeva; but when she talks about her ideas, my mother never uses her name.

When we talk this way, though, I always repeat a half-joke that she'll never be given a copy of the project, the book (this book), that she isn't allowed to read it. She's not fed up, exactly, but her small chuckle breaks off.

Well, why not.

I have probably led her to believe she knows what all's in it, the content, everything—and this could almost be confirmed by how much we've discussed it, hours every week, for a year. She doesn't. I don't talk to her directly about the abuse, about all the ways my ex-husband hurt and violated me; when it comes up, I elide as aggressively as possible so as to give her permission to do the same. I just tell her that many parts would be uncomfortable to read, given our emotional proximity, given how uncomfortable those parts have been to write.

Well, like what.

My family has done well in never acknowledging that he was abusive, that what I did was as much *survive* him as *divorce* him, precisely because I have ablated the whole thing, the sex and violence and the bodies, the archives of my violable body.

Well, what does that have to do with those videos and snakes and all this other stuff, that K person.

Sometimes, we want answers that don't answer more than we want explanations that do. So I say, *Well, the internet—that's what.*

She goads, and she calculates; she stops silent, voice still, and then the realization:

It's all on the internet.

I

WHAT IS THE POINT OF EMPHASIZING THE HORROR OF BEING?

—JULIA KRISTEVA

I've never dated, married, fucked a person in person, a person I met without that shine of LCD or LED intercepting us. When I have pined, in person, all saltburn, it has been for straight men, for people who may as well be more distant than that LED person, elsewhere. Because, in the cornfields, all men claimed to be straight men. First came the browser-based profiles on dudesnude, HotOrNot, OkCupid, Adam4Adam; then the apps, Grindr, Scruff. These have been how all my romantic relationships were initially facilitated.

My mother's worry, informed by I'm not sure what—news reports of the dangers of these (dating) websites—instilled a shame that kept me from admitting my use of them when I'd announce to her that I would be going on a date or, later, when someone would ask how we met. Using these sites and apps was once *reckless*, *irresponsible*, and *dangerous*. Now, when some people ask, my partner barks the flippant answer, *Scruff* (although it was really Grindr, the imagined twink version that has seemingly dropped in popularity since our cultural fetish for hyper- and hyperbolized masculinity in the gay community has swelled), smiles almost belligerently, and enjoys their unknowing faces as they refuse to ask for elaboration.

■

Once, writers were all taught that there are certain words that don't do anything, that are always inferior to the whiteness of the action verbs insisted on by the *show, don't tell* era of the discipline. Out of this, we've come to consume less poetry than fiction, and we especially like stories and dramas in which characters *shoot*, *walk*, *eat* rather than just *am*, *have*, *think*.

I had been trying to write a research journal, a list of entries documenting my hours spent sleuthing for a document online, when I realized it was too difficult—not the sleuthing but the documenting, not writing about the internet but just writing the internet, this thing physically before me, even now as the autosave wheel spins, without any substance or action. The problem is that the actions, the drama of this search, this *hunt*, happening on the internet, happening somewhere between me and the screen, culminate only to *scroll*, *sit*, *tap*, *watch*, *read*, *masturbate*, *swipe*. Besides, I have more thoughts to *tell* than I have actions to *show*.

A stuffy, bearded professor once said to *write what you see*, although this quip is no more helpful than the other: I'd presumably write about computer, television, and cell phone screens, but to *write what I see* would necessarily describe my relation to it, all the ways my thumb tapping and mouse clicking manipulate it.

A third option, from yet another professor: *Write what you know.* The problem, here, is that I don't yet know how to write a surfeit of still images that won't stop moving.

■

This, my current writerly kind of life: A professor, hired as mentor to me and those like me, tried to mold me into this recognizable thing, this person who'd be more like *him*, all *write what you know* documentarian. Driven by what must be my chronic oppositional defiance, I did what I perceived to be the exact opposite. I began writing what frightens me, what I refuse to know or admit I know. The opposite, the underside of a document.

He had no language, no advice to give me to write the internet and its cacophony of multiple feeds, multiple profiles, the eternal connectivity, the sleuthing, and the unforgetting. He and a group of other professors told me to read books by people who are *like* me—which I think means *queer* or irreverent or vulgar or, indeed, oppositional defiant, a possibly offensive choice of words for how it makes their authority compulsory.

So I did. I looked for answers from writers who write about the body, the internet, and maybe, hopefully, how the internet relates to the body, how uncomfortable that is. We spent months developing a reading list—a long one but, nonetheless, just *a*. Where I began didn't seem to matter, so I eased myself into it, going with something I *know*, something familiar. I went with queer; I went with Chicagoan; I went with nothing they had suggested; and it was just that quickly that I began to find answers—from the mentors I found rather than the mentors I had been given.

Reading for this project started in earnest with T Fleischmann's *Time Is the Thing a Body Moves Through*. Only three sentences in, and there's mention of the internet, a hookup app. Scruff. Only much later is it described, and insufficiently at that, as *one of those tap-tap apps*. (They write, elsewhere, that to *describe something* distances us from it, and indeed, it would be insincere for millennials to distance themselves from the internet, their phones, or the apps on them.) The verbs remain those small pseudo-actions in this text, *tap*, *look at*, *keep checking*; both the internet, as in the virtual space itself, and what we find there are just objects. Perhaps the simplest relationship there can be.

■

Whether these verbs are interesting or not, others still catch my eye: Fleischmann writes about blips—avatars and map pins that *travel* and *follow me*. The subject for these, the doer of the action, is data, light and triangulation, binary. There is no human agent, but there is a subject that nonetheless bears upon an actual physical body as object. Theirs, mine.

The actual life, that is, *physical* life, that Fleischmann describes in *Time Is the Thing* is one in which writers and artists all know each other, all bump elbows in a grid, collaborate, and inspire. They call it a *loosely accumulated trans social fabric of activists and artists*—an urban kind of life, by necessity, a kind we've seen before in our histories and cultural imagination: very much like an American Bloomsbury Group or 27 Rue de Fleurus or, only a ten-minute walk away, 55 Rue de Rennes.

(And what does this become, a life like this, during a pandemic, when it is stripped of its social nature—except it never *can* be, can it: The Minneapolis and George Floyd protests, the protests against police brutality, had the highest turnouts in American history, pandemic be damned.)

■

For a long time, I lived a rural life that barred me from the kind of life in *Time Is the Thing*. Once I moved away from home to a suburb (closing in on urbanity by degrees), I tried this life, tried to get it, have it. I seemed to have it: smoking clove cigarettes after a burrito dinner (vegan, vegetarian, organic) on someone's roof deck, talking about a poem by Mary Oliver with the woman from Austin who had never seen snow. This couldn't be sustained, though, for a number of reasons: money, jobs, summer, relationships. Then, once I got to Chicago, I *couldn't* have it: Urban living kept me so broke that my days mostly consisted of walking to get cash advances and selling old electronics to pawn shops and calculating food purchases according to SNAP's $1.50-per-meal budget. *Walk, hock, budget*. Then I found myself married to a man who drank all my savings, prevented me from having friends, and sabotaged anything that might have been for me that was not also for him.

■

Later still, and elsewhere, another attempt: I asked my friend, D, if they knew Fleischmann's work and recommended *Time Is the Thing*. It'd complement their work on Appalachian writers, I thought, because the author is from Tennessee, although, I said, I knew them primarily as Chicagoan, like me. I knew them *as a* Chicagoan, like me—although I really only *knew* them through Scruff and train stations and literary grapevines, which, of course, isn't *knowing* at all.

The book comes up in conversation often—it occupies a space in the corpus we've developed as both friends and perpetually *budding* scholars. We refer to this literary figure, this public specter, as Clutch, even though their Amazon author page identifies them as T, even though both their books are published under the name T, although that initial is always there. But in articles, interviews, and blogs, that initial is always followed by Clutch, as if T is the author of books, while T Clutch is perhaps a persona, an existence captured by a net of web pages. Clutch, I think, must be the human addition to the initial T.

We use *Clutch* for the same reason we use *Dorothy* for Dorothy and *Jenny*, Jenny; *Kim, David*: We very consciously aim our insouciant hyper-valuation of familiarity and intimacy at those who let us *bud* but never *blossom*, who hold us to a *more appropriate* register—as if everyone doesn't become someone else when they are transcribed onto the page anyway. Our embodied languages insist, *We will not be made in your image.*

This attempt at a writerly life may just be an attempt at a younger one.

■

A very long time ago, whole lives past, I was asked which superpower I'd rather have, flight or invisibility. How silly, I thought, how unexpected for a professor to ask me this. Is it normal for a professor to want to know me, me, as a person. (No.) *Invisibility.* No question, no hesitation, and not something I hadn't already thought about: It's the only thing that could ever save me from my greatest fear, which is discovering only too late that I'm being watched—my recognition of that unflinching gaze from wherever it comes. Yes, invisibility would prevent that gaze from ever falling on me, but, more importantly, invisibility would allow me to see whose gaze falls upon me.

My answer, I knew even then, was also an immature hormonal desire. Of course I'd wanted to gaze without inhibition, a desire exacerbated by straight men not wanting me to see anything, wanting my gaze on anything but them. And what could I have seen. There are videos like this, of course, spy porn, videos shot through peepholes of men on the toilet masturbating quietly to whatever is on their phone, unaware of being seen. These are more arousing than the similar cruising videos, in which the participants touch, suck, fuck, willing to be seen, whether or not they know they are.

More arousing: the urinal spy shots in which the person's awareness of the gaze is ambiguous, despite the probability that he is aware of the urinal divider's failed promise of privacy. Most arousing: that moment when the man in a green T-shirt sees that he is being seen and turns himself toward the camera to be seen better—the way he matches our gaze, then follows it back down, then up again, and grins so widely, happy or flattered instead of angry or embarrassed—the way he just zips up and leaves.

■

Fleischmann describes themself as lying between two other bodies in a hot summer bed. This is the verb, the action: They lie there, the three of them, each on Scruff. Fleischmann comments on how they, these three users, appear as a single row in the grid displayed on their devices. What they do not mention is that the order of avatars necessarily changes by device—our own always displayed upper-left-most, depicting the virtual space relative to each user's body, rather than as an objective representation of a reality where we occupy the same equal space on that bed in a particular order. We are shown-not-told how these three relate rather than how they relate to the digital (*sit*, *look at*, *tap*).

They describe the trio as *comparing the men with whom they occasionally chat* and how this goes on *for hours*.

I've had several Scruff profiles shared with me, across the table, at the bar, in bed. This is often precautionary: *Does he look like a serial killer. Would you fuck him. Have you fucked him. Is he good. Can you believe. Is this your ex.* But sometimes, this is cruel. Sometimes, it is evaluative in a different way: when my ex decided for us that we wanted to have threesomes, when my ex decided for us that we were open, when he told me that we were now poly, when my ex decided that he could fuck anyone and that I would fuck no one—profiles were *compared.*

What we compare, when we *compare men,* is not limited to the public profile or the information accessible to any one of us sitting on that bed with Scruff open and in hand. There's nothing to *compare* if we are all looking at the same static profile.

No, certainly most of what we compare when we *compare men* is *not* public but is instead the messages and locked albums, the *good morning* pictures of us in bed and the *if you open the door this is how you'll find me* pictures of our gaping asses. It is this information (a word that suggests the binary doubles as something akin to *fact*), *unique* information, the private kind that we share. DMs and unlocked photo albums are *private* only to the person who reveals them—*private,* an apparent euphemism for *shameful.* It's the *dirt* we want and the *grit* we compare.

■

Just as often, when a different crowd asks how we met, when my partner abruptly answers, they respond *Oh, cool* without missing a beat, any flippancy defused. It is the truth, even if some would rather not hear it shared. Scruff mentioned early and often in *Time Is the Thing* is quotidian—apps, and our engagement with *these* apps in particular, are compulsory, incessant—not nearly as radical and exciting as I first read it. This is like that *grit* or *dirt* that makes our dramas and fictions seem more realistic: No novel ought to be written in which nobody shits or masturbates. I don't believe in a movie when nobody pees, drools in their sleep, or says the wrong word. Life is predominately all that, and I do not see the point of censoring it.

This same notion was expressed by Mark Marek, the owner of a shock site, after being charged with corrupting morals. He said, *I established BestGore so the information that is routinely censored by the mainstream press, is available to those who are interested. . . . Those who want to see reality ought to have access to content that exposes it. After all, real life is uncensored.*

Another shock site, Ogrish.com, teased us with the tagline, *Can you handle life?* The site was passed from owner to owner several times, rebranding each time, and eventually left us with a current goal of becoming *a respected media outlet for uncensored, unbiased news.* Both BestGore and Ogrish hosted the same media, mostly atrocity.

■

We may think that *comparing men* simply means sharing information about different people, but it may also be that we have different information about the same people—a Venn diagram of message histories. My palms sweat as I read *Time Is the Thing*, because I realize that, even though I never messaged Clutch on Scruff, mine may still have been a profile compared, my avatar and *good morning* and *open the door* photos. Both paranoia and reasonable suspicion—likelihood does not matter here.

But how trivial: This is what these apps are for. We *sit, look, swipe* as subjects just as we insert ourselves as objects into the same space where we may be looked at, tapped, swiped—inject ourselves into a community without physical space and so without bodies, and almost none of us are exempt from this. Even something as innocuous as an email is a way in which we demonstrate our addressability, that we want to be addressed, that we invite communication. Signing up, logging on.

This is also what exposes us to hurt. In *Citizen*, Claudia Rankine quotes the philosopher and gender studies scholar Judith Butler as saying, *We suffer the condition of being addressable.* So what would be the harm—do we ever really think we (our bodies) aren't being seen, as objects, objectified.

■

Americans' right to privacy is largely a myth. There is precedent in which we find an *implied* privacy, only something indexed by and somewhere between the First, Third, Fifth, Ninth, and Fourteenth Amendments. Possibly because of property laws and again, now, with digital information laws, we imagine an innate division of public and private. Despite how this imagined privacy may have protected us, laws and rights may apparently be reinterpreted at any time.

When we are in public, we should have neither the expectation of privacy nor any assumption that laws are in place to protect this imagined concept. The picture I take of your exposed torso is mine, private; your body, public. The picture I take of your gray sweatpants is mine; your bulge, public; the index of your penis, public, even if the organ itself is private.

This is the principle behind CreepShots, both a website and its own search term or category on many others. Users say to *use stealth, cunning, and deviousness* to capture our *target*: These are, ultimately, candid images of people (women) in public, images that sexualize the person (woman), that document sexual appeal—images that depict our (men's) desires when we no longer desire the surfeit of porn star bodies, always already nude and ready.

The premise of this voyeurism is more disturbing than the images themselves, which are almost all PG and SFW: Creepshots are violative; they are harassment images, taken surreptitiously and without consent. At times—the upskirt images, the *See Thru* category, the nude beach photos—they feel *more* sinister; like that gaze, the camera or lens is maybe more than metaphorically penetrative. But these *fetishist freaks*, these *perverts* who participate, are largely innocent. They may get charged for being a public nuisance, maybe for harassment or stalking, but never for anything related to the privacy you don't have.

The sharing, the *comparing* of creepshots is supposedly for male bonding, for advancing and uniting under some hegemonic masculinity. That's a polite way, I think, of saying *rape culture*—a culture that apparently transcends even corporeality.

■

Our gaping asses, our *good morning* and *come find me* images are sent to only one person. That's an intentional limitation set by the software: We are granted a *public* space for images as well as locked folders, *private*. Whether these images, once sent, are private or public doesn't matter, because in this virtual grid—just as in our physical, waking world—privacy is an imagined concept. Instead, what matters is consent. Public images: I consent for these to be seen, not by everyone, but by anyone. Private: I will grant access to these images on an individual basis, one individual consenting to one other's gaze.

So sharing that dirt and grit, these images, when we *compare men*, sidesteps that consent, violates it. And maybe conversations are different—maybe in a one-party consent state, this is fine, because the recorder is consenting to having their own conversation recorded by themself, and maybe this applies to screenshots as well. But all those times a cell phone was passed down the bar with a *Check this guy out*, image full-screened and zoomed, I think two people just violated that *guy*'s consent. Those times my ex turned his phone to show me, to ask me, *What do you think*. The laughing and derision when you show me from across the table, *What the fuck is that*, and I lean in to inspect what I think you think is disfigurement.

The *private* image, the image I send to *you* and not to *them*, is one I own (*private*, then, as in property). It is also an extension of *me*, my violable body, which, when in public, is public.

■

How would Clutch react, then, reading this: that when I saw someone on the train platform in Chicago who matched, who looked similar to their author photos I would turn my attention back to my phone only to see, in the grid of Scruff in my palm, CLUTCH. So simple, how the digital can not only corroborate our perception but also confirm our suspicions.

We call this *creeping*, creepy. But I think it only can be when we are caught, when the behavior is recognized. But no one could have known. While I have always had a kind of physical referent for them, a knowledge of the antecedent, the body behind the binary—author photos, email signatures, Scruff—I'm certain that I was always unknown, if not anonymous. My faceless body, my lack of celebrity, and a Scruff username and photo (headless torso, like so many others) that could not correlate the profile with this person—it made me invisible to them, just another body in an urban density that makes everyone a vague nobody.

Regardless. I know I am better able to stomach the idea that I was a voyeur than the idea that this could be, *is* recursive—seeing each other seeing each other see, binary writing itself into existence between us, this mise en abyme of gaze.

■

Learning how to write the internet, the horror of it, this simultaneously physical and ethereal thing, has demanded that I change my reading habits. My mentors and advisers want me to read books by people who are *like* me, who they say are like me. I already read books by people *like* me, and they point to others who are not like the authors I read. Genres I don't read. And suddenly I am aware that these people do not—indeed cannot—perceive me the way I perceive me. My focus, my study, shifts for a month or two: I can come back to Scruff and the internet but right now I need to see how I am being seen.

I've read myself through the list of books I'd been given, and I've come somehow to a book triangulated by but not on that list: Mattilda Bernstein Sycamore's *The Freezer Door*. Here, in the acknowledgments: *and T Clutch Fleischmann for reading the manuscript at a later date, and so thoughtfully adding their important insights in key areas.*

Neither *T* nor *Clutch*. T Clutch, the author-person.

I feel instantly both like and unlike Sycamore. Like, because here is another Venn diagram, a web of connectivity: a small little family of people who look at and toward each other with similar interests. Like, because when Sycamore mentions a person in the acknowledgments, I know who that person is.

Sycamore's life, which I'm inappropriately conflating with the life of *The Freezer Door*, is like Fleischmann's, like the life in *Time Is the Thing*. And this makes me feel *unlike*: because these lives are similar. I've called it *the writer's life*, compared it to Woolf's and to Stein's, but, in *The Nation*, Becca Schuh goes so far as to describe Clutch (T)'s as the literal archetype, the *blueprint* for this *personal community of socially and politically progressive individuals, an anticapitalist pocket of artists and activists, sex workers, and practitioners of direct action.*

I don't know what I am supposed to learn from reading books by people who are supposed to be like me but are only like each other except that I am not *like* either of them, or both of them. Any of them, actually.

This is of course an anxiety that Clutch and Mattilda (Eileen, Wayne, Maggie, the rest) were invited to a life and community that I never will be, that my queer body is not progressive or threatening enough for me to even be queer, that I'm not good enough at being queer, that I'm not good enough to even be queer.

■

My family jokes, at my mother's expense, about how the three children were raised: My older brother watched *RoboCop* religiously before he was even ten, and when you are raising three children, the younger is plopped down next to the older in front of the television. So, just as my brother sat with our sister, five years older than he is, to watch *Pretty in Pink*, so too was I plopped down next to him, religiously watching the violence, the disgust and sense of shame at the dismembered man in that suit. My mother offers *The Fly* as another, as her favorite example.

And yet, I was expressly barred from watching *Dumbo* and *Bambi* for how they completely undid my brother. The thought of losing Mom has proven to be far more psychically damaging than the brundlefly pulling Geena Davis's shotgun to its forehead—or, later, Sigourney Weaver's mutated plea, *kill me*.

All three children, though, loved *Labyrinth*. (If you were here, I'd also ask, *You want me to recite the whole movie, with sound effects and songs, from beginning to end, because I can.*)

My brother, just now, sends me a meme depicting two children of the late eighties/early nineties in front of a television, enraptured:

7 YEAR OLD ME WATCHING JASON VOORHEES BEAT A WOMAN IN A SLEEPING BAG TO DEATH AGAINST A TREE

When the family rented *Dracula* (the one with Winona) (the one with Keanu), I was asked to leave the room, to step into my mother's bedroom during a sex scene. I peeked, of course. I remember breasts and confusion as to why there were so many bodies.

Sex and loss, both taboo; but not blood, not death, and certainly not the violation by a facehugger, the horror not of a chestburster but of discovering the man we thought was human was an android all along.

After my sister moved out, my brother and I watched movies at night, after Mom went to sleep. I'd sit on the floor or the edge of the bed in his darkened room, and we'd watch mostly horror films: many slasher thrills like *The Texas Chainsaw Massacre* or the *Halloween* and *Friday the 13th* series and probably just as many psychological horrors like *The Shining* (what is that bear doing), *The Haunting* (the good one, not the bad one), *Cube*.

The films I loved the most, and what my brother and I eventually settled into, was a particular blend of body horror and something else I couldn't yet describe: *RoboCop*, *The Running Man*, *Total Recall* (perhaps it was Arnold himself who interested me), *The Thing*, *Blade Runner*, *Brainscan*, and every *Alien* movie (even the one with Winona) on repeat.

■

Gatekeeping used to refer to gay men pushing lesbians out of the community, to the struggles of getting medical care, housing, public restrooms for trans folk, to bi folk being considered only *half gay*. And, in my experience, it applies equally to a particular brand of queerness imagined as *LGBT-squared*, queerness as enlightenment, a queerness that Venn diagrams the spectrums of sexuality and politics. I'm usually shocked, made a little sullen by interactions with queerfolk who have occupied this progressive anticapitalism: I am a *slut shamer* because I said I wouldn't choose to risk chlamydia by having sex with someone while they have an active infection. I am a *repressed prude* because I expressed my disinterest in being poly. My vote for Hillary proved me to be obdurately *conservative*, which made me, in turn, tumultuously un-queer. I've learned that, according to many, queerness has certain visual markers and geographical ones that I don't have, that it demands a certain quota of volunteer hours and a mandatory number of days spent with picket signs and an independent voter registration.

So I feel excluded: I'll never be queer enough.

■

I once dated a progressive anticapitalist who taught feminist theories at a college just into the suburbs. When we'd flirt and kiss on the couch, we'd use the quiet moments in between to talk about art and literature and feminist theories. We had that in common, reading. It wasn't out of the ordinary, in those squished moments, for him to say something like, *You'd love Kristeva.* He said he was surprised that I didn't already know her, given my interest in film, in Sigourney Weaver and the *Alien* franchise, in J-horror, in theorists like Judith Butler. He often left me speechless and unknowing, silent and guessing.

Perhaps because it was so embarrassing, it's easy to recall the frustration of the post-date googling—every different phonetic spelling I could imagine of *Irigaray* and many other names he used when we discussed his work, my work, gender. By our next date, I'd have read enough of Wikipedia to at least respond, pretending to know something I did not, something about the way lips touch or never do—doubles and halves.

Feminist Theories assumed I was as well-read as he or otherwise felt that he didn't need to dumb himself down for my sake. Although I later convinced myself that I appreciated this, his intelligence, his jargon brought out my long-repressed or corrected stutter. In an attempt to sum it all up, he said, *Kristeva—it's about the horrors of the mother, like how everything in* Alien *is a penis or vagina, and how that guy is pregnant with this little alien, and it, itself a phallus, bursts through his stomach. And it kills him.*

I mean, I guess that that that that sounds like fun, I guess.

■

What if, despite all this anxiety and politics, I were brave (*good*) enough to be more like Mattilda, to ask Clutch for their input or feedback. They are addressable, so why not:

> *Hi, you probably don't remember ever emailing me those couple times, but I do—about how neither of us have any real social media presence, about essays, this blog—and here is this imaginary book in which I write about writing about you and also looking at you—and maybe we can call it creepy but I prefer to think of it as resourceful, Scruff just an iteration or extension of Wikipedia—will you read it and offer feedback so I can put you in my acknowledgments so that I can be more like Mattilda, because I'm being told to be like her, like you, and I just don't know that I am.*

■

One of the ways I have evolved into my current queerness has been by being visibly (limp-wristedly) and audibly *gay*. I have always *sounded gay*—those verbal mannerisms and that inflection. Maybe in second grade everyone teased me because this part of me became more noticeable. Or maybe everyone started teasing me because my speech already drew attention to itself, whether I sounded gay yet or not.

I went to speech therapy for years. My impediment was not so severe that my family can't joke about it now, when we watch home videos—the one where I'm standing in our backyard under the willow tree and am asked to sing a song. *Fink-ol, fink-ol wi-do twa.* Mine was also probably the *least* severe of those who were in therapy with me—all of us pulled out of our regular elementary classrooms every day, reading with each other, large headphones on our heads—at least two of whom still had an impediment by graduation.

After my peers became hateful bigots and bullies and then (some) finally outgrew it, or at least stopped pointing it at me, after I got braces and expanded my palate and got retainers, after being told years later that I didn't need to wear my retainers because my wisdom teeth will come in and shift all my teeth and I'll need braces again anyway, and after I went to the dentist for my wisdom teeth pains (rotten, impacted—all) and discovered I didn't have dental insurance and couldn't afford the procedure outright—after all that, my teeth shifted, and my bite opened. By the time I finally was insured, ten years later, it was already too late: My antiretroviral therapy had caused so much bone loss that insurance wouldn't cover even a simple cleaning. The cheapest and only option was to remove them all.

The thing is that *gay voice* isn't marked by a lisp at all, but rather by an over-articulated sibilant. I overcame my impediment, mostly, but I'm still self-conscious. I want to believe I *sounded gay* then because speech therapy taught me to over-articulate *everything*—indeed, my mother often reminds me how well I speak—but my sibilants now whistle, regardless, for how my fake teeth don't rightly fit together.

An insufficiently queer lisping, limp-wristed body.

■

Kristeva treated a boy, Paul, with delayed speech—the goal, for him to come into language. He couldn't, because the semiotic and symbolic (language) are sequential, so she sang to him, sang with him. They made up songs together. That is, she worked with him in rhythm, tone, and melody (the semiotic) until he gradually came to speak, in language, more and more frequently.

(What, then, of my own juvenile singing.)

■

I could not have known on the couch if I liked Kristeva, but I thought I liked the idea of her—the idea of her ideas, the idea he had of her ideas.

When I asked about it, the book, the theory, in my doctoral program, at work, my professors and my colleagues said, *Everyone has heard of Kristeva* or *Everyone knows abjection theory*, which left me stunned silent and stuttering: I hadn't. I don't. During all my time in the Ivory Tower, no one even mentioned her name until I myself came with it on my lips, until I started asking. Maybe this is gatekeeping too: the academic equivalent of *iykyk*.

I feel *unlike*.

Yes, and I was told by as many people—those who help me to sound smarter and more qualified than I am to apply for jobs—that *Not as many people know who this is as you think* and *How many people do you think will understand all this.* The student is always wrong: in this case, incredibly wrong both for not knowing *and* for believing *everyone knows*.

■

My position in academia is, as it were, a queer one. I have had some successes in it, and I am, verifiably, on the *inside*, now supposedly sheltered from the *dirt* and *grit* of the outside world by a few pieces of paper.

What I and those like me hear from the inside, though, is

> *Congratulations, you're a doctor and professor now, and your knowledge and expertise will still never matter, not if someone (a man) has been here longer. Congratulations, you're now an expert in an area that is actively unacceptable here, unaccepted by your seniors; therefore, you are not an expert at anything at all. Moreover, because your expertise is in something unrecognizable, you've never had any expertise. Lucky for you, though, your seniors would be happy to* undo *you and imprint themselves upon you. Congratulations, by the way—we won't ever die, so there are no jobs for you here. You can go work in the stables.*

The Tower, *this* tower, is built on seniority, compartmentalization, and abuse. These principles effectively make an outside of the inside: a waiting room with dusty plants and *Maury*, a gallery exposed to the elements, a doghouse in the backyard, a sealed-off mudroom. A coach house, at the very best.

■

My doctoral program, especially, was a four-year relationship of abuse (just like we have all been saying, and yet):

Least senior and newly hired faculty inflicted their academic hazing rituals upon us and attempted to throw their imagined weight around: *You are wrong, so let me repeat the correct answer, which is the same as you said, except it's mine.* The program suffered the frenetic ineptitude of at least one nepotism hire meant to teach in a discipline and genre for which they had no practical experience and even less demonstrable knowledge. Their being ignored by the most senior faculty, its own abuse.

I am young, uncomfortably young for academia. I studied too many things as well as nothing of import (creative writing, always the weakest link in an English department; the essay, the fourth genre). Too critical to be creative anyway. I don't stand behind the lectern, I refuse to match their tone, register, or tenor, and I refuse their thought-terminating clichés of *This is just how it's done*, *Back in my day*, *You don't understand*, *I know it isn't fair, and yet*.

Like every other program, I think, when sexual assault occurred, the department's primary concern was to protect the assailant as cheap labor (who else could cover all those English 101s when everyone is so busy teaching their *one* upper-level seminar for ten students or going on sabbatical). Title IX and the police department, our only avenues to protect ourselves from each other and our faculty, were always already failing us: not only setting the burden of proof so high that even a specious claim, evinced or otherwise, can throw the whole investigation, but also developing definitions of abuse, hazing, assault that require kinds of evidence that are always already considered moot.

If academia is a tower, I think it is more Branch Davidian than Ivory. It's a cult: interpolated, indoctrinated, brainwashed, abused. Always a leader, and it will never be you. Believe or leave. Inside/outside—just a matter of perspective.

■

After years of Wikipedia and blog posts about it, I bought her book, *Powers of Horror: An Essay on Abjection*, and read it unsuccessfully.

My partner, now, tells me that, until I held the book in front of him, he had heard *Kristeva* as the author's full name: *Chris Teva*.

I show him the cover, the picture of Julia, *the* photo of her, the one where she looks off to her left, lips parted, hair swept by the wind across her forehead, slightly wrinkled by her raised eyebrows. The photo is beautiful, captivating if only because of that parted lip. The photo is obviously staged, we can tell by the placement of her soft, ringed-fingered fist on her jaw, but somehow *unlike*: She is not smiling, not looking at the camera. She seems more like the subject of a Dorothea Lange photograph than a movie star, as many authors seem to (try to) portray themselves, so many either moody black-and-whites or Shirley Temple poses.

We commented on how sad she looks, although, anymore, I can't see it. I can't picture her as being sad ever, at all. She is one of the few theorists I have seen a video of, and she walked out on stage and sat in a chair there in front of a large audience. Rather than sadness, when I look at the photo now, I see the way she eloquently and graciously apologizes to the audience in English for the ineloquence of her English and the way she smiles, bright pink lipstick and large blue sunglasses. Despite the black-and-white photos of her, despite the supposed horror, the depression and disgust surrounding her, she is, as a person, bright and colorful and pleasant.

■

My notes and underlining in *Powers of Horror* were done diligently and intentionally, not only because I would *love it*, as Feminist Theories told me, but also because I felt such pressure to read and to understand. How could I ostracize myself from that *everyone* who has heard of *Chris Teva* and her theories. It was a labor, that first time, and a chore, and maybe I didn't understand much of it; but, either because I was already in the cult or because I saw it as a test of loyalty to join, I wanted to understand all of it. And I needed help.

It's embarrassing to admit a failure to understand, humiliating, perhaps, to know we do not know enough. That's why I never did admit it, not on the couch when I talked to Feminist Theories. A simple, *Yeah, which one is that again* is enough to elide the fact while also soliciting enough information to participate in the conversation.

This, one of the tricks of an academic, of academia—this ability to never have to say *I don't know* or *I don't understand* or *It's better to ask someone else*—all far too close to *I'm wrong*. We can't be held accountable for the prophesied and passed apocalypse; we simply pivot toward another.

Well, I'm not sure about that: This emphasis implies we *are* sure but that what the other person has said is not part of what we are sure about. For the inside, a generous correction; for the outside and the initiate, being told they're wrong.

I'll check my bookshelves: We attempt to signal that we do in fact have the knowledge, even if not readily available. It is effectively a statement of priority, synonymous with *I'll get to it later*. The time between, the delay, I think, is when we google our phonetic spellings and read Wikipedia. For the inside, confidence; for the outside, a denial of access.

Yes, but and *Yes, and*: We play the couple's therapy game by beginning with an affirmation of what the other has said. We are bad partners, though, because we usually just add on whatever we *do* know, relevant or otherwise. For the inside, a redirection; for the outside, an evasion.

It seemed to me that, by and large, if they were not purposefully withholding *Chris Teva* or guarding their expertise, then there wasn't anyone around me who could help me understand or give me the resources to understand. (There is no *Chris Teva for Dummies*, no lay version, no version that doesn't operate as if *everyone knows* already.) (Trust me; I have looked, and I have read many that claim to be this version.)

■

One thing I read again and again in these many books on Kristeva's theories: At least outside philosophy, many will acquaint themselves with her and remain interested for only a short while before moving quickly on to another theory, never to return. Over and over again, these books tell me that we, that *everyone knows* her name better than we know her thought. So while everyone will claim the importance of Kristeva's theory of abjection, according to her experts, in practice, it's a fad.

In fact, in the English departments I've experienced, K and her theories have been supplanted. The touchstone for abjection is not its author but is instead a book on only a sliver of the abject in film: Barbara Creed's *The Monstrous-Feminine: Film, Feminism, Psychoanalysis*. It is predicated on the assertion that men fear misbehaving women. It's about order and staying in line, things that women and their bodies don't have or don't do according to the male gaze of Hollywood. So these are our monsters, and this is what makes a horror movie. Look, vagina dentata; look, Carrie's menstruation; look, remember what Regan did with the crucifix in *The Exorcist*.

Feminist Theories' own interpretation of K, I eventually realized, was only a hasty recapitulation of Creed.

■

During my poor urban years, I walked up to Howard (once, then, even a bus pass cost too much), and, for the first time, I walked into one of those large, flat single-roomed spaces obviously built for other purposes to get a payday advance. I walked through row upon winding row of retractable stanchions to arrive at the teller windows. I gave that money to my ex because we couldn't afford his drinking, and he wanted to go out that night, but I wouldn't come. Because I didn't like watching him watch other guys and their partners. Because I didn't want to be asked to go into the restroom with him, hoping for something sexual but instead just to be hit. Because I was tired, he thought. And I was. So very.

Eventually, he decided that advances were insufficient and that we needed *extra* income, which should come from webcamming. Now, a performer can use multiple accounts to cast simultaneous shows so as to have multiple available lines for tipping, but that wasn't an option for us then. We both had to do the work.

He had moved into my apartment. He was set up in the living room, and I was in the kitchen. When it became clear that my room was getting no traffic, which I did not mind, it also became clear that his was getting much more. Jealousy got the better of me, and I created a second account and joined his room as a guest—not anonymous, but not noticeably *me* either. Suddenly, the wall between us became insubstantial, and I could watch what he was doing and, in a way, pretend he was doing it for me.

I didn't bring in enough money for him, and masturbation, it turned out, wasn't lucrative—*mine* wasn't—so he told me that he would now be fucking me on cam, and I refused, and he did, and I said no and so that is what we continued to do regardless.

■

What I loved in *Alien* was never Creed's *archaic mother*; I didn't care about what had become of Regan's body in *The Exorcist*. I'm not scared by the opposite of order and staying in line (misbehaving). The horror that drew me in was, instead, the distance from which the violence was enacted upon Regan's body, a whole plane of existence away. The horror that drew my focus was the sentience of the android, the consciousness enveloped in a completely prosthetic body. I grew up thinking about genetic manipulation, bionics, and the small mouths inside us—that's what disturbed me, and that's not really the opposite of anything.

The movies I watched with my brother encroach upon what I now know to call *cyberpunk*, this high-tech and low-life aesthetic. The genre moved into the mainstream as we conceived of, invented, and implemented the internet—the historical context of my youth.

Academics were excited by this *new electronic frontier* and its ability to collapse fantasy and reality—this imaginary, imagined, unreal space that runs parallel and contemporaneously to our own tactile and haptic spaces. We can exist in this other plane, *you* and *I*, but our bodies, these vehicles we carry with us, these houses of self and identity are unwelcome. We developed new *terminal identities*, a term coined by Scott Bukatman for both its adjectival and attributive senses, both *slowly dying* and *a point of connection*.

Perhaps coincidentally, his corpus matches perfectly my brother's VHS collection. He looks at *The Fly* and *Alien*: Look at how our bodies are just these fragile things, these corruptible, mutable objects. See how we ravage them and dig through them and find nowhere in there a trace of ourselves. The self, continually displaced. See, then, how we are bound to exist beyond our bodies as *virtual subjects*, as Jeffrey Sconce observes in *Haunted Media*, *liberated from social markers of gender, sexuality, race, age, and class*.

Look how empowering. How queer.

■

The site of and obsession with the *hyperbolized flesh* in such films are what Creed should have us imagine when we reflect on K's theory of abjection. Our fragile and mutating flesh *is*—and is the only thing that *contains*—what K calls the *chora*, an imaginary space untouched by signification, language, and where infant cries, babbling, coos, and first almost-words mean something, somehow. We call this the semiotic, and it's what we master before we master language.

We can neither suppress the semiotic nor grow out of it. It's always there, churning underneath or inside us. It will break out, it must, but until it does, our obsession with flesh is an anxiety that we will spill out of ourselves, an anxiety that our flesh can stretch but is only so elastic, like a scab succumbing to a squeeze.

Bukatman and others observe, though, that we never do. Our selves never spill out. This means, he suggests, that the *body is not requisite* for a self: Subjectivity has nothing to do with the body—look at RoboCop, transplanted.

■

As our technology grew exponentially and we increased our use of and reliance on the internet, two things became clear: first, that we can or do exist without or beyond our bodies; second, that doing so is still a technological impossibility. Regardless, we delighted in the potential of our virtualities, unafraid even as we approached the imminent destruction from Y2K—a possibility that made it all so much more *punk*.

■

Write what you know.

Long before Feminist Theories, I would drive an hour and a half through the cornfields to spend weekends watching horror movies with a man I loved. He was an irrefutable cinephile, and that's what we had in common, movies. The first we watched, *28 Days Later*, begat other horror films which begat others, a slow crawl through his impressive DVD collection comprised of things I'd never seen before: bizarre stop-motion, Criterion Collection, Lars Von Trier, Japanese horror.

What I *know* is that there's another story, another history. In our march toward the awe and fear of a virtual event horizon, we were a step ahead and lonely. Japan, I discovered, has historically been significantly more technophobic than other countries, especially those in Europe and North America. In 1993 Japanese households were beholden to stand-alone word processors, and only 12 percent of them had personal computers. But it wasn't until 1999, while we were trying to decode digital rain alongside Neo and Trinity, that the Japanese public took interest in the internet: The first large-scale mobile internet service, i-mode, was launched by NTT DoCoMo.

What I know is that, only two years later, internet access reached critical mass in American households; and I know that, the following year, Hollywood released *The Ring*, a remake of Japan's 1998 *Ringu* (リング), itself based on Koji Suzuki's 1991 novel, about the girl in the well and the haunted VHS.

(This is what I *know*, because this is what I *saw*.)

Although it had obviously been viewed by many, Americans did not receive the original film or a translation of the source text until 2003. Aside from our own Hollywood interpretation of it, we hadn't seen anything like it in the mainstream—so different was the aesthetic, the perspective, the view of technology.

What I *know*, this time in a more primitive way, like intuition, conviction, is that, while we rewatched *Blade Runner* and wrote idealistically about the possibilities, the new frontiers of the budding internet,

Japan was suffering higher levels of technophobia that manifested palpably in their horror films. Maybe we couldn't hear them, maybe we didn't want to, but this perspective was somehow omitted from the echo chamber of academic positivity about virtual subjectivity. This is what led us to the self-evidence of our potato bodies.

■

With Cinephile, I watched all of these J-horrors, except one, *Audition*, for its slow burn; and the one that resounded in me, clung to my arteries, perhaps more than even he ever did, was Kiyoshi Kurosawa's *Kairo* (回路).

I can't recall the event of watching it, the way I do *28 Days Later* or his Sean Cody DVD, but I know we watched it in his basement bedroom, there, across the hall from the hoarded room with the computer, the cathode-ray monitor. I know that I was so terrified I cried, unable to move my back from the wall behind us, and that all I could say afterward—and the thing I kept repeating, even years later, when I described the film to others—was that *they just know something we don't.*

As problematic as that sounds to me now, I think I may have been right, in my own naive way. I couldn't name it, then, but the fear that I felt at the film was entirely encapsulated within a sadness and discomfort that I had never experienced before.

And once I developed the language for this, I didn't use it.

■

In *Kairo*, ghosts use the frequencies of internet connection as a portal to manifest themselves in our world. As a result, the living become desolate and despairing, literal shadows of who they were. Tokyo's population is decimated as individuals suicide or turn into black mold where they die or into ash before dispersing into the air.

Most of the scholarly readings of the film are the same, perhaps, as Jeanne Marie Kusina observes in "Difference, Repetition, Disappearance, and Death," because it is so obvious, so easy: an allegory on how technology is ruining society. Technophobia. The readings all discuss Kurosawa's oeuvre, how the visual framing by window casings and grilles reflects the characters' growing isolation. They all discuss how people *fail to connect*, despite the population density, and thus lose community and tradition. They all claim Kurosawa's vision is apocalyptic, and that this apocalypse is not without hope (look, there, a romance). They all reference the same four scenes, two primary sources, the same single interview with the director, and overall too much Deleuze for my taste.

But, unlike Hollywood horror (the slasher), the horror (both Kurosawa's and most J-horror) of this film is to do with how we exist, or don't, in the world. Ontology. Technology isn't a boogeyman; instead, the coincidence of the ghosts appearing and the living disappearing makes it seem as though our dependence on technology has us abdicate and forfeit our bodies. How queer.

■

Perhaps like Cinephile, I have been unable to get anyone, aside from romantic partners, to watch *Kairo*. Maybe it has to do with J-horror's rise and very sudden fall in popularity—our ability to *know* each one for their tropes before even seeing them. *It's a horror, but*, I say. I describe how it depresses, how it imposes. It's not sad, although, like every other story I love, everyone does die by the end.

■

Like the rest of J-horrors, *Kairo* too was adapted by Hollywood. Western marketing translated both the American release of the original and the remake as *Pulse*. I don't know Japanese, but it seems to me that this title, the translation, fails to capture what I understand the

Japanese to mean. 回路 is two characters, Kanji: 路 (*ro*) means *road, path*, or *way*; 回 (*kai*) means *to circle, to go back, to turn around.* It has been adopted into modern Japanese as a noun, meaning *any circuit in which energy or matter moves in a cycle, such as an electrical circuit*, but may literally mean something closer to *way back, back road*, or *come around again.*

Our translation *pulse* maintains only a vague sense of that circuitry in secondary definitions—*a transient variation of quantity, such as electrical current or voltage; an electromagnetic wave or modulation thereof*—but the word overwhelmingly refers to our arterial systems, that rhythmical throbbing of blood. What translation affords us, in this case, is a metaphor, maybe, a figuration in which we are each both process and production, both flesh and electrical emanation. Living, once, and coming back around again.

The Hollywood *Pulse* uncritically accepts that generic technophobic reading and marries it to their now classically post-9/11 American vision. In the remake, the ghosts *take your will to live. Everything that made you* you *is gone. You don't want to talk, you don't want to move. You're a shell. And then come the bruises. They spread all over. Your body dies right out from under you, and the next thing you know, you're just a pile of ash.*

In this context, our will to live is connected to our (American) individualism. The ghosts come to our world through the internet to take this from us—not because they need or even want it but only so that we are robbed of it. They are malicious: Their only purpose, it seems, is to turn our bodies to ash. They are hijackers and terrorists. It's easy to see how the internet's sudden rise in popularity and people's newly observed disconnectedness are being met with anxiety in this adaptation: *Our relationships have been reduced to texts.*

■

These ghost characters of the remake are in stark contrast to the spectral objects that are pushed here by physics in the original. Perhaps the only significant similarity comes when the main character, Mattie, receives email after email from her dead boyfriend, Josh. Because his account was still logged in on his computer, he was *present*—his existence seemingly still possible through digital communication with the living.

Being logged in used to mean we were alive and present, but being logged in is just a subject's current state, *constituted by electronic technologies and the machineries of the text*. From Mattie's perspective, Josh is both dead and present. Here and not-here. Josh's body, irrelevant—ash.

■

K started developing her theory of selfhood, of subjectivity, in her first book, *Desire in Language: A Semiotic Approach to Literature and Art*, and it wasn't fully developed until eleven years later, when she published *Powers of Horror*.

To start there, with *PoH*, as I did, can only ever result in a surface reading of K and an uninformed understanding of the content. Whatever I thought abjection was, whatever I thought that word meant after struggling through the book—all that I understood was rhetorical or only grammatical or algebraic: There is this thing called *abject*, which is neither *object* nor *subject*. $A \neq O$. $A \neq S$. Fine. But how can anything not be either of these. How is a dead body not an object, how is the skin on milk not an object. Why would something (*A*) ever be more threatening to me (*S*) than my literal opposite (*O*).

The most disruptive misconception is that hers is a *theory of abjection*, when it is instead part and parcel of a theory of subjectivity—like we are studying the Holy Ghost without any knowledge of the Trinity or have never even heard of the Bible. *PoH* is only the conclusion of an idea explained over seven books, all on subjectivity. And, for K, this has always been about language: We are subjects because we use language, because we speak.

Abjection is the true failure of language.

■

In *Time Is the Thing*, Fleischmann says that, while they sense its importance and possibilities, they *fail to understand* the digital space: *Our human bodies can be haptic tools of whatever lives in a thriving digital space, as I understand it, and this could be revolutionary and/or a nightmare.*

According to Fleischmann's assessment, the digital space is linked to our bodies—there is a direct and immediate correlation between their body and the square avatar always in the top left of Scruff; bodies and the digital space have reciprocal agency and control over each other. They think they were *too late, even if only by a few years, to fully appreciate and live there*, in this space *where language and bodies do something different.*

They are only a couple years older than I am. (I know that they don't have a Wikipedia or a social media profile that would tell me their age, but I check anyway: When you search for T FLEISCHMANN WIKI, Google spits back Tomáš and Trude and Bernhard and Chuck. If you add CLUTCH to this query, it gives you only T.) But if they are right, that they missed it, then I am presumably one of those who *live there*, who *do* understand, who *appreciate.*

Unlike.

I live *here*, alongside the internet, with it, more like a sibling than a house—an entity I've grown up with, not a *space* at all.

Maybe it is only those a few years older, only the older generation, who view *Kairo* as a simple technohorror, and maybe this sentiment is also the reason why the film fails to connect with the youngest generations, as Wooju Chong claims in "The Fleeting Nature of Techno-Horror." This horror is particularly millennial.

■

When dial-up connected the majority of American homes to the internet, it became not just a possible vehicle for folklore, like home remedies and urban legends and conspiracy theories, but it became folklore itself—became our cultural knowledge, a way of knowing and seeing; a place we could find, make, maintain community, united by values and beliefs and interests. It was a queer horizon, and we were suddenly untethered to our geographies. It infected our waking lives and corporeal relationships: *Have you seen. Did you read. You should go to this site. Here, let me pull it up for you.*

The same year *Kairo* was released, the internet gave us TubGirl, the cultural meme, the image of a woman in a tub with her feet behind her head shooting a laminar flow of shit up out of her ass and down into her mouth.

This, the *thriving digital space* Fleischmann is in awe and terror of.

■

In *Kairo*, our first protagonist, Michi, works at a plant nursery, Sunny Plant Sales. In the greenhouse, she approaches her coworker sitting at the phone. *Still no answer at Taguchi's*, she asks. *It shouldn't take a whole week to work on that disk.* He must have his reasons, and maybe something's wrong, but we also discover from another employee that *If we don't get that disk now, we're in real trouble.* Michi suggests she goes to Taguchi's apartment, to *see if he's okay*, to *see how he's doing.*

When she arrives, there is no answer to the doorbell, so she enters using a spare key from under a flowerpot—containing a long since deflated cactus. Here, the movie title screen: a full-body shot of Michi from behind. We zoom in to medium as she shuffles items on Taguchi's cluttered computer desk. In the other room, she pulls floppy disks out of a hamper and from off a dining chair. She pulls a cloudy vinyl curtain back, and we find Taguchi in what must be his bedroom.

Hey, you are here. This seemingly addresses her invasion, but the lack of emphasis in the hardcode subtitles and my inability to hear such emphasis in Japanese makes it possible that it means something else entirely. Like a reminder.

Regardless, pleasantries, then, *Did you finish working on that disk.* While grabbing an Ethernet cable, he says, *It's somewhere in that pile,* pointing beyond the camera, back at the desk where we opened.

Michi looks again for the disk while, in the other room, Taguchi hangs himself.

Is it the one marked Work File. Taguchi.

When she sees his body, she falls backward, fetal, bringing a sheet up over her nose and mouth.

■

Later, still reeling from that trauma, we watch through the window of a café, Sweden, as Michi says to her coworkers, *Oh, I forgot. Here,* and places the disk from Taguchi's on the table for Yabe, the one who cautioned them of the approaching deadline.

Back at the nursery, Yabe goes to the office computer and opens the contents of the disk. Moments later, he asks Michi and their other coworker, Junco, *Would you take a look.* With all three in front of the desktop, he opens an image from the disk. Almost immediately, they recognize it's Taguchi's apartment: the same messy computer desk with two monitors we saw Michi rummage through earlier. In this image, a person stands in the room, facing the messy desk. *Is that Taguchi.* They look closer and see that the primary computer monitor in the image shows the same image—a camera pointing at its own feed, Taguchi caught there and replicated by the mise en abyme. Michi points to the other computer monitor in the image. *That's a face. A reflection.*

This is the face of the person standing in Taguchi's apartment, facing his computer. The reflection is indistinct, and the image itself is unclear, as we would expect: a reflection on a computer monitor as captured by a webcam a whole room away. The nose is the clearest part of the image, and there is a blackness encroaching upon the hair and ears. I think if we could just manage to see the eyes, we'd be able to tell who it is, but blackness spreads across these too, altogether hiding them along with the brow, which stretches the nose up indefinitely between two empty sockets. Maybe Taguchi, indeed; and maybe not.

We are repelled by not only this unknowable face but also a cognitive (and maybe emotional) dissonance: This image was *just* taken, Taguchi only *just* killed himself, I *just* saw him, he *just* died, and yet he *just* appeared, just now, *here* rather than where we saw him. Look, the now-dead Taguchi is alive again; simultaneously, now-dead Taguchi is still dead.

■

Portraiture used to be mimetic, representative of the actual human stuff sitting before the painter. The belief was that a person's essence, their subject, the spirit correlated directly to the uniqueness of their face. We believed in physiognomy and phrenology: Chaucer's Summoner's narrow eyes, *black scabby brows*, and *whelks of knobby white* or Whitman's *animal will* and *large philoprogenitiveness* and *size.*

That is, we once believed we were a united thing, body and self—an incorporeal being nonetheless wrapped in flesh. Then some insufficiently Surrealist portraits caged that same being and tested the flesh, pulled it taut and almost transparent.

The first time I could have seen Francis Bacon's work was in Tim Burton's *Batman*: The Joker and his cronies break into the Gotham City Museum and knock over, spray paint, stab sculptures and paintings, vandalizing almost everything. Joker sees one of his knife-wielding henchmen approach Bacon's *Figure with Meat* (1954): He raises his cane to stop the slashing knife and says, *I kind of like this one, Bob. Leave it.*

I don't know when I came to *recognize* his work, though, or how. It could have been through this movie—again, plopped down with my brother to watch a favorite—but it could just as easily have been during those hours I spent in the queer (*LGBT*—it hadn't yet been squared) section of Half Price Books, looking for a life I couldn't yet live, and discovering how his father tried to beat Bacon's sexuality out of him. Or during all that time spent browsing the art section, looking for things I wasn't supposed to see, that *artistic* nudity that never mattered to me, at that age, beyond the errant nipple or the silhouetted erection.

I stood, three times, in front of his *Figure with Meat* (1954), displayed in the Art Institute of Chicago. It depicts Pope Innocent X, seated, framed by racks of meat. His face is—what. Not unclear, exactly, but distorted and made imprecise by brush strokes and hues. Representative, perhaps, but almost indiscernible. The institute describes Bacon's figures as *tormented* and *deformed*. While the image appears deformed, I don't think the subject is. I think of him as moving—just fragmented and not yet contracted into a perceivable being, like he was too soon or has since become long gone.

Describing his *overall concept* for his portraits and *concentrations of reality* in "The 'Visual Shock' of Francis Bacon: An Essay in

Neuroesthetics," Semir Zeki and Tomohiro Ishizu explain that many recognize the *merit* of Bacon's work, but supposedly few describe it as *beautiful. Almost all* viewers *find them disturbing.*

■

Throughout our cognitive development, we establish templates for what we encounter—invariant aspects of what we come to consider a group of things. It's how we come to recognize and to discriminate. As we grow, experience, learn more, the templates become more and more forgiving and flexible, malleable—to the point where something altogether foreign still kind of fits.

Very early, though, we establish a template for a human body, and we can't quite stomach violations to or deviations from it—especially a face. When we encounter one that is violated or so foreign that it doesn't follow the rules of faces—we cannot ever adapt to this. It is a *threat to identity*, our own—it is the epitome of what K calls *abject.*

As if victims of some violence, Bacon's figures have also been described as *disfigured* and *mutilated*, *pitiful* and *terrifying.*

■

I used to believe in the phrase *I think, therefore I am*, thought I knew what it meant for Descartes, this phrase that seems to have been confused with and by *mind over matter*. Who you are is a *thinking* thing more than a *physical* thing; and that thinking thing, our minds, consciousness, or reason, has primacy over the physical thing, the body, the *stuff.*

In 1949 philosopher Gilbert Ryle describes this dualism, Descartes', as a mistake of category—apples and oranges. The mind and body, he reasons, cannot be discrete *substances* when the mind has none:

> *A person's thinking, feeling and purposive doing cannot be described solely in the idioms of physics, chemistry and physiology, therefore they must be described in counterpart idioms. . . . The human body, like any other parcel of matter, is a field of causes and effects, so the mind must be another field of causes and effects, though not (Heaven be praised) mechanical causes and effects.*

Mental processes and physical processes have no reason to be conjoined or disjoined. That contrast between them, between mind and matter, subject and body, must be dissipated.

I don't know if this is an answer or not, but psychoanalysts don't seem to fall for Chaucer's characterizations, and many, like K, refuse to exactly follow our Cartesian heritage of the self, identity, the soul, mind—any of it, whatever we call it—this *dogma of the ghost* always already ensconced *in the machine.*

She and other psychoanalysts all look to a short few months of our infant development, between breastfeeding and speaking, as the time during which we develop a self, our subjectivity, begin to exist as subjects, as selves—a time in which the *ghost* manifests:

Roger Caillois and Paul Schilder say we cannot develop a continuous sense of self until we can develop that spatial comportment: We cannot know *who* we are until we know *where* we are.

Freud says our ego, at this time, is a mental projection of what we see in the mirror. We are just our surfaces, flesh and clothes and spittle.

Lacan says the baby sees a whole baby in that mirror. That image of a self, though, is distinct from my self—I am alienated from it—because we only ever perceive ourselves in bits and pieces: limbs, senses, desires, spittle. We are fragmented, but the mirror image, the mirror self, is not. To correct that dissonance, we conjure a fantasized image of wholeness that we can never achieve.

Yes, and. K says, during the same period, the baby turns away from the nipple during nursing, creating, for the first time, a disunity between itself and its mother. That is, our mothers are not us, and our mother is *there*, *that*, so what are we now, if *not* that, there.

(I've seen Reddit arguments about the ableism and heteronormativity inherent in all these ideas. The responses vary wildly, but at their core is this weak and timid assertion that the problems are manufactured by the reader, the student, the critic: The mirror is *not* (necessarily) literal, the fragmentation is (hopefully) *unreal*, there doesn't *have* to be a nipple, much less a mother. These are our *counterpart idioms*.)

In many ways and many times, K insists that the body *is* a requisite for the self, that the mind is predicated upon matter. The contrast between them is moot.

■

This pubescent period of the internet saw many shock sites crop up: Rotten.com went live in 1996, Ogrish.com in 1999. Many were standalone, featuring only a single *shocking* thing, a single video. One of the first I remember was "2 Girls 1 Cup," shared with me by my college roommates. It's a one-minute clip from *Hungry Bitches* (2007), directed by Marco Villanova and starring Karla and Latifa, who shit into a cup, eat it, and vomit onto each other.

This would be an example of what many would have me believe is *abjection*: disgust. *Feces is abject*—that is what my mentors and colleagues can muster. This, and *Are you familiar with the skin on the top of milk. It's like the corpse.*

A video like this does certainly elicit disgust.

Shit is gross, fine. But if we struggle past a surface reading of *PoH* (as I remember my own), it becomes clearer that what we deem abject is, as K says in many ways, multiple times, that which transgresses limits or collapses borders. It may *result in* repulsion and disgust, but it is ultimately distinct and different.

Of shit, specifically, K writes: *Contrary to what enters the mouth and nourishes, what goes out of the body, out of its pores and openings, points to the infinitude of the body proper and gives rise to abjection. Fecal matter signifies, as it were, what never ceases to separate from a body in a state of permanent loss in order to become* autonomous, distinct *from the mixtures, alterations, and decay that run through it.*

Every time I read K, I struggle to parse meaning. I must do it slowly. Every single time:

Contrary to . . . : Unlike what we eat, what we expel *points to* (but is not) the limitless body. What's already clear, here, is that shit causes abjection. Thus, *shit* and *abjection* are concomitant but not equivalent.

Fecal matter . . . : Shit represents what we never expelled as we became subjects, who are *distinct* from the stuff that happens to (and the non-nourishing stuff we put into) our bodies. When we established ourselves (*me, I*), we simultaneously established *not-me* as well as *undoes-me*. Subject, object, abject. So shit reminds me that I did all *that* kind of expelling.

So the abject is about limits and borders, yeah, but those are a product of subjectivity (language, for K).

There's a fine, thin, translucent line, a limit, a border between, on one side, this system of metaphors that allow for our subjectivity—arbitrary relationships between the actual stuff that comes out of our asses and the sound of the word *shit*—and, on the other side, the semiotic, the *chora*, all those ways we articulated—shitting, for example—before we became self and subject.

We can't afford not to be in the symbolic, so we maintain this limit and border to keep us from falling back into this space where we stop existing as ourselves. We always need *shit*, but we can never afford *to* shit.

■

Incidentally, our language is only designed to *tell*; to *show* is an impossibility.

■

Yabe receives a phone call where the caller on the other line repeats *tasukete* (*help me*) in a small distant voice that crackles with internet connectivity. When he pulls his cell phone from his ear, he sees displayed that same photo of Taguchi standing in his apartment. So, if dead and still communicating, then. Then tension. The dissonance registers in us, but not in Yabe. Instead, perhaps because he exists in a *real world* as opposed to observing a *fictional* one, he acts logically: He goes to Yabe's apartment to investigate what must be a technological error.

No one's there; computer, unplugged. He continues his search for clues. We brace ourselves for when he clicks on the lamp in the other room and relax when no threat appears over him, around him, behind him as he digs through the clutter. Behind some computer equipment, he finds a piece of paper with only a few printed words, folded and crumpled, that has fallen there:

HOW TO MAKE THE FORBIDDEN ROOM

■

This is the boundary, the limit, the division with which K is concerned. Abjection has to do with the collapse here, the failure of the symbolic: *When the condensation function that constitutes the sign collapses (and in that case one always discovers a collapse of the Oedipal triangulation that supports it), once the sound image/sight image solidarity is undone, such a splitting allows one to detect an attempt at direct semantization of acoustic, tactile, motor, visual, etc., coenesthesia.*

Okay. So.

When language fails us, we revert to *direct semantization* by making sounds and gesticulating. That is, we are reverting to the semiotic: *A language now manifests itself whose complaint repudiates the common code, then builds itself into an idiolect, and finally resolves itself through the sudden irruption of affect.*

The boundary, the inside/outside (*me/undoes-me*) of abjection theory, is a metaphor; the body is a metaphor: *The body's inside, in that case, shows up in order to compensate for the collapse of the border between inside and outside. It is as if the skin, a fragile container, no longer guaranteed the integrity of one's "own and clean self" but, scraped or transparent, invisible or taut, gave way before the dejection of its contents.*

Because our metaphorical body is *fragile*, when language (the thing that makes me *subject*) fails, it opens, and all the *not-me* stuff comes out.

When *shit* stops meaning shit, we are split between the symbolic and semiotic, between language as sufficient and language as dearth. Our only *language* now is affect: rage, disgust, fear, humiliation. Look at how easily the body gives way to this and our insides come out to make *shit* mean shit again.

The most opposite to my subject is not an object, like my scraped and stretched flesh. What is most opposite to my subject (abject) is, instead, the fragility and weakness of my skin. I'm not undone by seeing the body's insides; I'm undone when I see that my body/language cannot keep the *chora* (not yet subject) away. Knowing that *I* is *you* and everything means something—this doesn't erase the fact that, before, nothing meant anything.

So maybe "2 Girls 1 Cup" is abject. If it is, though, it isn't for the shit.

■

The corpse is the *utmost* example of the abject. This is what K says and what is so easily repeated by those *everyone knows* individuals. The corpse is *both human and not human*, death infecting life. It's easy to see how people interpret this to mean that abjection is a confrontation with mortality, that it is the *utmost* simply because *it dead, me alive*: *A decaying body, lifeless, completely turned into dejection, blurred between the inanimate and the inorganic, a transitional swarming, inseparable lining of a human nature whose life is indistinguishable from the symbolic—the corpse represents fundamental pollution. A body without a soul, a non-body, disquieting matter.*

So ambiguous, fine; but, more to her point, we are subjects in and because of our bodies. The corpse shows us that a body is waste, a pollution of our subjectivity. We can't stomach the possibility of being undone, of becoming an *undone-me*. Maybe the translation isn't as precise as it could be: The corpse isn't the *most opposite ourselves*; it is, instead, the most opposite of *our selves*.

■

"2 Girls 1 Cup" became so popular, so known and pervasive, so evident, that the title has become meme, formula, an index of shock content, of agency and intent:

1 BOWL 1 SLAVE
1 GIRL 1 PITCHER
1 GUY 1 BRUSH
1 GUY 1 COCK
1 MAN 1 JAR
2 GUYS 1 STUMP
1 GUY 1 NAIL
1 GUY 1 MOUSETRAP
1 GUY 2 SPOONS
1 GIRL 99 STOMPS
1 BOY 2 KITTENS

A fuller list reveals only three possible themes: homosexuality, sodomy, and castration; coprophilia; and gore. There is not much distinction between these three. There is no evolution here, no shift from porn to violence, from same-gender attraction to blood. Instead, these images and videos we lured each other into seeing have always also been brutal and disturbing: It was the same year we saw "2 Girls 1 Cup" that "3 Guys 1 Hammer" was leaked.

True crime author Brian Whitney claims that this video of the Dnepropetrovsk maniacs, as they're called, *wasn't meant to be seen by anyone but the killers* (hence, *leaked*): *To them it was a personal keepsake, a trophy so to speak, something for these lunatics to get off on when they are sitting around the house with nothing to do, when they weren't busy killing people.*

Whitney offers no receipts.

The word *leaked* is visceral, suggesting something of the fragile body, humors and other fluids. Something pointing to *the infinitude of the body proper*. The word means that there was not permission, that it should *not* have been disseminated. The fact remains that someone intentionally uploaded it, which necessarily means that one of the assailants intentionally distributed it to at least one person outside their group. Private, public.

I can't decide if "3 Guys 1 Hammer" is shocking because it is abject because it depicts murder or cruelty or is just something we weren't supposed to see—and then, if because it is illegal or because it is illicit. Because someone dies or because someone kills.

■

When I call to discuss this project with my mother—when she and I create this imaginary book in which I talk about subjectivity (which, with her, I refer to as *selfhood*) and the internet, how we position ourselves in relation to its archive, the detritus, and the illicit, and my frustration at knowing that, when K says *the corpse is the utmost of abjection*, she is wrong and that isn't the point anyway—every time we talk about this, it's as if she has forgotten our previous conversations.

My phone-call pacing is stopped abruptly by her long and disarming silence. I can't tell if she is silent because she is confused and processing or because we've disconnected or—and this is what scares me the most every time I sit to write this imaginary book—because this is a response to the disgust and judgment of me and the shit I've admitted, which is usually only the one thing I did in college just to see if I could, and I could, so I did, and I kept this fact almost entirely hidden until one night I dreamed of this imaginary book ostensibly about that sword, the slack jaw, and wagging tongue.

But she finally says, *All I know about that is that I watched this old movie, and it disturbed me so much. I can't remember what it's called, but I wish I had never seen it, because even thinking about it*, and she gags, audibly, over the phone, *thinking about it makes me want to puke. There's this guy tied up in a chair, okay, and some other guys put some contraption in his mouth to hold it open, you know the sort of thing, and—and you know how gaggy I am anyway, my whole life, I can't even go to the dentist without gagging*, and it's true, she can't, so they pour a packet of salt on the back of her tongue to shut off that mechanism, *so maybe this is all to do with having a small mouth or something from my childhood.*

She suggests that all this, all this *stuff* I spout off, about this theory and that, these theorists as if they are real people, as if they are people who matter, as if theory matters—this is all certainly subjective, that my problem with the fallacy of K's corpse actually isn't to do with anything that I've said at all; instead, the problem is that there can't be a universal *ab-ject*, as she pronounces it—no possibility that one person can speak about and for all humanity.

She's right; I know she's right.

My mother's, *her* abject, this scene, is horrifying to her because of her own small mouth and the way she gags when she opens it, even to brush her teeth. She's convinced that I have, as always, overcomplicated: The problem I'm talking about, with the corpse and abjection, is—*forget all that*, she says—*the problem is that everyone is going to react to it differently. Wouldn't the corpse be* less *abject to the coroner.* I tell her that some may even delight in a corpse and that K calls these individuals *corpse fanciers.*

All this is to say, I think my mother gives very little credence to this kind of capital-T theory. And it doesn't seem to me that many people *are* interested in theory, like this: My partner listens to what I say about Chris Teva, I solicit opinions and examples, and what I get in return ranges from *Okay* to, in an exaggerated yokel accent, *I don't know about all that smart people stuff.* My friend D listens, generously, and comments only on everything that isn't the theory itself.

I would describe this as avoidance, prejudice, or explicit bias—like broccoli or snakes or race—if I couldn't see how theory doesn't *want* to be interesting or popular or appealing or even understandable. It is the discourse only of academia, made intentionally inaccessible to those outside. Why would anyone actually be interested in this kind of theory. And why am I.

■

Here's how I think this goes: We teach theory, any theory in particular, because we are taught that it is important, and we don't question that (we aren't smart enough, yet, to be allowed to ask questions). Indoctrinated, we then say things to our own students like, *Everyone knows Chris Teva* (even if we don't) and discourage *them* from questioning the importance of the thing we are teaching. (This is essentially academic hazing.) This is a discourse, it's indoctrination—the Ivory Tower is a giant phallus, and teaching theory is masturbatory at best. Like any other form of power, it is designed to be self-sustaining, reproducible: Ascribe and you shall be granted a modicum of that power; the only alternative is to abdicate and rescind.

The other way this can go is: People use theory to demonstrate the fragility of that tower (now more di Pisa than Branch Davidian), to either mock or to undo the ableism, the sexism, the heteronormativity, the whiteness, to be up in arms about Freud (who, and I'm speaking as a once-rural citizen here, is the only capital-T theorist anyone actually knows, which probably explains much of the bias).

■

This irritating question: *What does your partner teach.* There is almost always a shock or disbelief that comes with discovering I am not partnered to an academic. *Oh, I don't know how you could do it* or *It's great to be able to schedule our classes around. . . .* I bite my tongue, because my job is not yet secure enough to be flippant or to honestly express how I feel.

■

I wrote a seminar paper on Jennifer Kent's *The Babadook*, a film about a bad book, a mother, a monster, a child. In the research, I saw a prolific use of the term *abjection*, and the references to K were many, but I noticed immediately that most were from only the first chapter of *PoH*. The numbers in parentheses never went up, never went higher than 15 (never), so, then, K's appearance in my writing was only *For further analysis, see*—yet another way academics refuse to admit they do not know or, in this case, do not yet understand.

"Approaching Abjection" is the chapter everyone cites. It begins with her poetic impasto of abjection, which remains undefined, and ends with a description of its applications in religion and in the works of Dostoyevsky, Proust, Joyce, Borges, Artaud. At its end, K refers back to this chapter as a *phenomenological preliminary survey* of abjection which will be given a more *straightforward consideration* in the following chapters. This means that, when we cite these first fifteen pages, we intentionally cite work that is intentionally broad, imprecise, or admittedly unclear. We are *explicitly* told in the title that the chapter has not yet gotten us to abjection: We are still only *approaching.*

Perhaps I was not the only one unprepared for K, opening this notorious book with only my Wikipedia knowledge and supported only by a collective knowledge that *everyone knows Chris Teva*. Perhaps we choose to cite work that is intentionally imprecise, distorted, or admittedly unclear because, after page 15, the text becomes too difficult. Her writing, especially in this chapter, *is* difficult: Her prose is a net of aphorisms and anaphora made almost indecipherable by the strings of appositives in virtually every sentence. Perhaps we cite these pages precisely because her sentences *are* equivocal. Take the very first in *PoH*: *There looms, within abjection, one of those violent, dark revolts of being, directed against a threat that seems to emanate from an exorbitant outside or inside, ejected beyond the scope of the possible, the tolerable, the thinkable. It lies there, quite close, but it cannot be assimilated.*

A *revolt* is directed *against a threat*. But is it the *revolt* or the *threat* that is *ejected*. And from what. Is it the threat or the revolt that cannot be assimilated. Or, worse, is she using the journalist's comma to elide what always seem to me essential words, not saying that the *threat* is *ejected* but that the threat is *of something* that *has been* ejected.

Now I know, from the rest of the book, that what *lies quite close* is the *threat*, not the *revolt*, the abject; and I know that abjection, the *revolt*, is a process, a verb, a series of actions, a means of becoming: To become who we are, we have all ejected the unthinkable, and we revolt against its continued proximity to us, of that threat of infection, infiltration.

■

As in the trial of the Dnepropetrovsk maniacs, of "3 Guys 1 Hammer," atrocity images are often distributed as evidence despite our wishes to avert our gaze: Exposure to these images, we think, corrupts our youth and morals. The images and videos are traumatizing. We imagine people wanting to *get off* on these videos, and indeed perhaps the maniacs did.

We refuse to be that kind of a pervert, and yet sometimes we *have* to look—courts and justice *force* us to—and at other times, we think seeing, watching, would be easier, perhaps better than a sense of unknowing.

When Mark Duggan was killed by police officers in London in 2011, the tension between Black communities and the police increased. His, another unjust death. The vehicle Duggan was in was pulled over in an area unmonitored by CCTV. It was reported to the media that there was an *exchange of fire*, and the Complaints Commission said Duggan shot first. They said Duggan shot the officer. Then they said that the officer shot first, that the bullet in his radio was a police bullet, not possibly from Duggan's weapon. Then it became clear that Duggan never fired. The vehicle was inspected elsewhere. Then the vehicle was returned to the crime scene for its investigation. Duggan's family wasn't informed of the incident, the murder, for days. Then in May 2014, Metropolitan Police Commissioner Sir Bernard Hogan-Howe informed the public that that same police force would be equipped with bodycams. *We find we're the only people at an incident who don't have a camera.*

In August 2014 Michael Brown was murdered in Ferguson. The officer fired twice at him through his car window, and he and his friend fled. The officer said Brown stopped, turned around, and charged him. The friend said Brown turned around with his hands up after the officer fired additional shots. Many heard Brown say, *Don't shoot.* The FBI had no evidence of this. Of the twelve rounds the officer fired, six of them struck Brown. Brown was unarmed, yet the court concluded that the officer acted in self-defense. Protestors demanded more body cams, and, indeed, millions of dollars were spent on exactly this.

In January 2023 Memphis officers pulled over Tyre Nichols. He was pulled from his car, tasered, and pepper-sprayed. He cried out for his mother, who was less than a mile away. Then he was beaten with fists and boots and batons before being pepper-sprayed more. When the medical team arrived, they did not assist or evaluate Nichols for sixteen more minutes—twenty-eight minutes after he had slumped down from the car, presumably having lost consciousness. He died three days later. The officers and the reports claim Nichols was stopped for reckless driving. They claimed he was violent, that he started to fight, that he reached for their weapons. CCTV and body cam footage disproved all these claims.

Eleven days later, Georgia officers raided a camp in the woods, a protest of the Atlanta Public Safety Training Center, aka Cop City. Manuel Esteban Paez Terán, one activist, was shot and killed. The director of the DeKalb County Medical Examiner's Office said the victim was shot twenty-seven times, while the state autopsy reported evidence of fifty-seven shots on Paez Terán's body. Georgia State Patrol does not wear body cams, but the Atlanta PD does. The footage from Axon Body 3 shows officers inspecting and tearing down tents, seizing potentially dangerous items. Gunfire is heard in the distance. Then more, so much more, so much faster. The officer asks, *Is this target practice.* How the video is compiled makes counting the shots difficult, but there were clearly more than twenty. The autopsy determined that Paez Terán was probably seated on the ground outside their tent with their arms in front of their body. The degree of force was used because, according to officers, Paez Terán was armed, uncooperative, and had fired at them. The autopsy cannot prove that they had been holding a firearm before being shot.

Evidence of atrocity can benefit those who want the truth, whether that's in the name of authority or justice. In a society that believes in facts, we all hope for exactly this, mimetic proof, because it can corroborate testimonies, prevent misconduct, and assign fault—millions of dollars spent at our request to decrease our (perceived) privacy in public despite our disgust at having our (only-perceived) privacy in public violated.

■

My father used to be a cop. During this era of civil unrest which came to a head in the *George Floyd protests*, a term I hate for how it seems to interpolate Floyd himself as the object protested—during this time and in reaction to a particular instance of police brutality on the news, my father sat there and, in a long, hesitant, and low, perhaps embarrassed voice, explained that an officer can't hesitate.

I don't think we've really reckoned with the fact that police officers use evidence of atrocity for training purposes, for education, with the fact that our society develops a particular skillset with this tool. While some of the training videos for law enforcement are of the poorly dramatized, stock-image ilk, others are dashcam footage of an officer's improper risk assessment—that is, of officers being killed on the job.

YouTube provides its own graphic or violent imagery click-through warning for the video of a police shootout from 1998. From the dash of the patrol car, we watch as a white pickup truck is pulled over, apparently somewhere in Georgia, at 5:33 p.m. A man gets out of the vehicle and steps a few steps toward the police car, his husky or German shepherd visible in the cabin. At 00:27, Deputy Kyle Dinkheller steps into frame, left, an arm stretched out toward the civilian. Dinkheller is on screen for fourteen seconds, standing near his vehicle, watching the civilian dance almost maniacally in the street. When the man runs toward him, Dinkheller retreats from frame. Twenty-seven seconds later, he returns to the frame for only five seconds, seeing, just as we do, the civilian open his truck door and brandish a gun. Dinkheller does not reappear in the video, though his voice can be heard. First, *Put the gun down.* Then the first shot. Then we see the windshield suddenly fracture. Then we hear Dinkheller's screams from the passenger side of the vehicle.

Years after the video was uploaded, user PaulCape commented, *This was the first video they showed us in our Weapons training class at the Greenville County Sheriff's in SC.* The students of that class, he explains, were told that Dinkheller had one *issue*: *He could not pull the trigger in time.* (*You can't hesitate.*) The point of the training, of watching this video, as PaulCape puts it, was not a lesson in weapons training or risk assessment but merely a condition of employment:

IF WE HAD ANY DOUBT IN OUR MINDS IF WE COULD PULL THE TRIGGER THEN WE NEEDED TO LEAVE THE ROOM AND FIND ANOTHER JOB

This unwitnessed, this implied and invisible atrocity, *haunted* PaulCape *for months.*

And then he went to YouTube to watch it again.

His comments have since been removed, deleted, or hidden.

■

The footage from the Nichols incident was released three days later. There was a countdown; we were promised it would be shocking. We held our collective breath, both for the moment we'd see the atrocity and for the public backlash to whatever atrocity we'd see.

There was the rage surfacing in us all about the event itself and another, separate rage at how the media made spectacle of the evidence. Emerald Garner lost her father, Eric, to police brutality in 2014. In that footage, we heard him repeat *I can't breathe.* She, alongside Reverend Al Sharpton, spoke out against our culture of spectacle: *The fact that we waited for this video to be released like it was an exclusive movie that needed to be premiered on a certain day—it really boils my blood.* She referred to our behavior as being like *a public lynching.*

■

Apparently, *many* former future officers rewatch these videos. MrMikesMondoVideo uploads almost exclusively this same type of dash- and body cam footage, with various pro-gun news reports and commentary interspersed. In the comments section for "Police Shooting—Constable Darrell Lunsford—Nacogdoches County, Texas" alone, users remark:

SHOWED IT TO US JUST A COUPLE DAYS AGO
JUST SEEN THIS TODAY AT MY ACADEMY CLASS
SHOWED US IN 1998 PSP CLASS 103
WATCHED IT BACK IN 1991!
WE STUDIED THIS FILM WHEN I WENT THROUGH
MA STATE POLICE ACADEMY IN 1993

Other comments vilify the civilians responsible for Lunsford's death, others mourn the loss. Some explain the lesson to be learned, however obliquely.

All of these have also been removed, deleted, or hidden, leaving only comments about the three killers being caught, then released, how they should be hunted and *pushing up daisies*.

■

One criticism of K's work, one of its *fundamental flaws*, is that the abject is *unthinkable*, a word she uses literally and without hyperbole. If that is so, these critics argue, she (and we) *cannot* think it. If it were true, this book would be imaginary.

This may explain why so many speak of K's work in terms of the corpse: Not only does it appear within the first fifteen pages of the text, but also she describes it as the *utmost* example, which essentially means that we don't have to imagine for ourselves any other examples. It is also one of the few concrete images K offers us. That is, one of the few *thinkable* images in those first fifteen pages.

If the corpse is abject, then the corpse should be *unthinkable*, but it is not, so she is wrong.

But we can actually *think* the corpse as much as we want. Again, what we cannot imagine is no longer being subject. $S \neq A$. The abject. When we do think it or approach it, we will know, because the semiotic will show up, *resolving itself through the sudden irruption of affect*.

But I hear them say, *But look, there, you just spoke it. If you speak it, you are thinking it.* We can, we do, because when we do, we are neither approaching a corpse nor the abject. Instead, we are positioned very far away from it, protected by metaphors, equations of sounds and images that ultimately mean nothing. Speaking the word *corpse* manifests nothing. Typing it, nothing is conjured at my desk. I am safe.

Again, *PoH* does not appear to be a theory of abjection at all, but rather a theory of subjectivity that is created through and alongside language—a matter of semiotics, signification, and semantics. *A disquieting matter.*

■

Despite his being a sexist and possibly homophobic pervert, I like Freud. I like Lacan too. Because I love language, and psychoanalysis is *all* about, is *fundamentally* about language.

It's a discourse in which the biblical Fall of Man (the lapse) is a metaphor for acquiring language, coming into this world of signs, the symbolic, as a subject (postlapsarian, fallen). The trauma of it is beautiful, how words deform reality, always already a failure of meaning—a *fetishist denial*, in K's words, because of how *the sign is not the thing, but just the same.* My words, these words, will never conjure the corpse, but, just the same, I (and you) conjure it nonetheless.

I am fortunate that *this* is how I was first introduced to theory—each its own metaphor or idiom to understand reality, each exactly as wrong as the next, although never really *right* or *wrong*, but just degrees of applicability. The dominant metaphor in psychoanalysis is not actually the Fall but is instead the story of Oedipus, who loves his mother and kills his father. But how ridiculous, wanting to fuck our mothers. How ridiculous, how homophobic of Freud, because maybe we have *two* fathers or already want to fuck our father instead. How ridiculous, the patriarchy.

But, even in psychoanalysis, Oedipus remains illustrative rather than definitive. Similarly, K does not say *every* infant turns away from the breast—except we all eventually do, don't we. She means *any* infant and, thus, none in particular, because there is no referent at all. There is no actual baby behind her words: We cannot watch our infant develop and say, *There, just now, look. Oh, could you see my child become a subject.* Instead, this story is chosen as analogous to how we become subjects through disavowal and this looming, uncanny force that threatens to smother me, return me to a state of being one with the mother—which means other than myself—threatens to undo.

These are just stories, allegories, myths. Theory, in this way, a new religion. And it does seem we treat these theorists as holy: We translate once, print forever, leaving the text untouched—as if the scholars and philosophers in the forty years since its publication never noticed the typo on page 9 or deemed it too sacred to edit.

But we do not have to believe it. And, moreover, I'd argue that if we don't believe, we don't need to be ejected from the Tower.

■

But, my mom says, *these people take this big snake, and they put it in his pried-open mouth, and it slithers down this guy's throat into his stomach. And it kills him.*

Now, the pause is my own.

Well, she asks.

I have never seen this movie, but by now I am familiar enough with my mother's description of the scene to know it is *Collateral Damage*. I don't remember ever watching it, but I did eventually google to find the scene: The snake is thin, venomous, a supposed coral snake fed easily into the victim's mouth—the only struggle being that of will rather than biology or physics.

My whole life, my mother's snakes have been big. She has these recurring dreams—she describes these recurring dreams with snakes. There are hundreds of them covering the living room floor. If they are fewer, then they are bigger. Sometimes, just a single big snake in the ditch, and when it's that big, it's always the yellow kind, the albino Burmese python. So when she describes the snake in *Collateral Damage* as a *big snake*, that's what I've imagined.

I confessed this to her, later, and she laughed. *How could a snake like that even fit down a guy's throat.* It couldn't, and that's part of why I've listened so enthusiastically to her description of it—each and every time she describes it to me. What she doesn't recall from the scene and the details she doesn't tell me have allowed me to imagine a dislocated jaw that exposes a wagging tongue to lick up the entire belly of some big constrictor whose ribs squeeze past teeth and under uvula, the stretched bleeding esophagus and the watering eyes, the pressure building behind there, the way retching would only open you wider for it, the horrible moment of being not only filled by it but also made elastic to accommodate more still, feeling this snake's weight both on you and inside you, *a weight of meaninglessness, about which there is nothing insignificant, crushing you*, and the way two bodies are first distorted to be made unlike themselves and then one is made the very boundary and limit of the other.

This scene is *all she knows about* abjection, so I listen for how *identity, order, a system* is *disturbed*, how boundaries may collapse—that threat, lying very near: Constrictors narrow and tighten us onto ourselves, and it doesn't matter, it turns out, whether they tighten to prevent oxygenated blood from reaching our brains or to prevent blood from oxygenating. Suffocation has nothing to do with air, only veins—something I learned from my legal adviser.

Her reaction, I imagine, happens in response to some very complex math done somewhere deep inside her: The snake is venomous, *black and yellow kill a fellow*, death creates a corpse (our own), and the corpse is a violent representation of what we have ejected to become subjects. It is the waste of our subjectivity. Death by swallowing a snake, then, represents the horror of the corpse inside that we have ejected because, now, we have language.

In my interpretation, her snakes *could* be abject, if she were born with them, with snakes living and churning inside her. The myth we'd tell would be like this scene, a story where we shut our slack jaws to the snakes that are always and at every moment wedging themselves between our lips. This imaginary book, then, would be about how the Serpent of the Garden is both the horizontal line of metaphor *and* the very script on its pages.

As I've grappled with the theory, with *all this stuff*, I've needed to delineate for myself what exactly is and is not, according to K, abjection. I've wanted black and white: One of our interpretations is right, the other is not right. But I'm just overcomplicating. *Forget all that.*

So, I do, and I say, *Yes, and.*

■

In *The Severed Head*, K writes about her own mother. It's a story about a radio show contest: The voice from the ether asked, *What is the quickest means of transportation in the world? Send us your answer, with a drawing to match.* Julia said *rocket*, and she was wrong: *"I'd say instead that it's thought," Mama proposed. I could only concede, but not without my usual smart remark: "Maybe, but you can't draw a thought, it's invisible."*

"You'll see."

I imagine a young K now, a pre–*Chris Teva* K, who sits in awe of her mother's drawing, tracing the lines with her stubby fingers, imagining this *invisible guillotine*: *To the left, a big snowman in the process of melting, his head falling off, as though severed by the invisible guillotine of the sun. To the right, the planet earth in its interstellar orbit, offering its imaginary expanses for armchair travels.*

She doesn't seem so abstruse now, seeing her essentially cheat to win a contest, pretending to know something she did not, relying on her mother for the answers.

■

The Dnepropetrovsk maniacs exist as a stark contrast, Whitney suggests, to Luka Magnotta, who by 2010 was keenly aware of the virality possible on the internet, on these shock sites. His record of violence and killing started with "1 Boy 2 Kittens," showing him place two kittens in a vacuum-sealing bag and their subsequent suffocation. In 2011 he uploaded "Python Christmas" to YouTube. In it, a cat is put in a Santa hat and tossed toward an albino Burmese python, which strangles and swallows it.

In 2012 he uploaded to kevin.666 a video titled "Time to Shake Things Up a Bit," renamed "1 Lunatic 1 Icepick" by the time it reached BestGore. Whitney's is the most detailed description I've read of the (apparently lengthy) film.

He reports that Magnotta repeatedly stabs and then cuts the throat of Jun Lin before he uses a kitchen knife to cut his flesh into fillets. Lin's head is held by the hair and his limbs removed. Magnotta simulates pleasuring himself with the limbs and simulates fucking the body. More filleting, then consuming, then feeding to a dog, then sodomizing with a bottle, then using a severed hand to masturbate.

Magnotta was hooded, and, of his face, Whitney writes, *I had no idea what was going on* with it, and indeed I recall a mask in the thumbnails. If my brother didn't once have the same item, I probably wouldn't have been able to tell that he wore a transparent disguise mask, the plastic kind with eyebrows, lips, and blush. The molded shape of the cheekbones and the entire mask's shiny plasticness change the shape of the face and distort its features, leaving an eerie contrast between the unmasked eyes and the blurry, hazy flesh.

Whitney suggests Magnotta *intended* for his killing Jun Lin *to be seen by millions*, that *the killing itself was meant to be secondary to the reaction the act would receive*, seemingly a satisfactory explanation for both the gross number of defilements and the simulation of others. Magnotta, however, claims he was made to do it, the film, the act, by Manny—that Manny uploaded it, that Manny's abuses were so severe that he had no choice, that he was afraid: *Sometimes when Manny was getting off, he would punch Luka in the head. He wanted to tape himself fucking Luka and would often ask Luka to do a threesome with him, so Manny could put it on the Internet and make money.*

Manny does not exist, though this does attest to the power of coercion and the horror of humiliation and the ease with which either of those can be fetishized.

■

When there have been lulls in our consumption of atrocity or boredom with our current shock sites, we have fabricated new ones. About the same time as I heard about our school's *pickle girl*, these same lunch-table friends, all in the corner of the cafeteria, told me about something called *stomp porn*, which was supposedly a woman crushing animals under her high heels. I don't think this is real. I think the closest we've gotten to this is breaking eggs under a stiletto in—

I was going to say *a music video*, but I couldn't recall if it was one by Lady Gaga or Brooke Candy. So I googled, and now I am aware that stomp porn *is* real—unlike *pickle girl. Crush videos*. There's a web full of people breaking eggs under their heels—neither entirely disturbing nor shocking but ambiguously sexual—and a series of videos a husband filmed of his wife crushing prostrate guinea pigs, worms.

Regardless, we do also fabricate shock sites: In 2020 YouTube user Feloista uploaded his video reaction to a supposed "2 Men 1 Girl 1 Supper." There are several of these reaction videos from the same year, and we can watch each person, sitting in a recliner or computer chair, laughing, retching, *oh my god*, squinting, covering their eyes. The video they supposedly watch does not exist. But by hearing the squelching audio and watching these individuals react to what's on their screen, we perhaps unwittingly triangulate it into existence.

■

"1 Lunatic 1 Icepick" became what it is today—that is, Netflix-worthy—while hosted on BestGore. Its owner, Marek, said in an interview with Whitney that the site is *nothing more and nothing less than a reflection of what really goes on in the world*. This statement is obviously true, but one that needs to be made regardless, for how some delude themselves: This video, this documentation of a murder (perception of documentation of murder), was treated as a hoax by authorities until, days later, body parts were delivered by mail throughout Canada.

Marek: *Pretending that it doesn't go on by not reporting on it will not mean that all that foulness does not take place.*

■

My mom says that my siblings are doing themselves no favors by limiting their conversations about death, about her death, by refusing to imagine it, by hiding it: *I don't want what happened to me to happen to them too. My mom hid it. She hid it very well. I think she thought that she would never die. And I guess I probably believed her. Now, everything is cut right in half. Everything after she died. And everything before.*

■

Michi, still shaken from Taguchi's suicide, washes the dishes as the news plays on the television behind her. The anchor reads: *A message in a bottle launched ten years ago by a boy on Tanegashima Island was recently discovered on a beach in Malaysia some four thousand kilometers away. Hikono Koichi was a fourth grader when he sent off his message. Members of a local group cleaning up the beach, a sea turtle habitat, discovered the bottle by accident.*

Even when we are anonymous, even if we aren't there, our utterances have a recipient. Steve Jones interprets the bottle story as framing *communication as somehow inevitable and futile.* This is part of how our subjectivity gives us language—or the other way around. The interviewed bottle-sender: *I never imagined it would find its way to some foreign country. I was shocked to get an answer after ten years.* Everything hinges upon being addressable. And then the story's over.

Next, the National Weather Service forecasts another unseasonably hot summer. It's the third for eastern Japan . . .

Here, the news anchor's face displays a two-dimensional glitch and becomes slices suddenly misaligned on the y-axis, like a corrupted file. Both the picture frame seen over his left shoulder and the window behind his right remain intact.

For Western Japan . . .

The audio, it seems, is affected too.

North Japan will . . .

Michi hears the audio cut out completely. She turns around to see the image on-screen stuck in a glitch: A black horizontal line runs through the middle of the anchor's face, right through his nose, the top of his head entirely missing.

It's an *improbable decapitation*, to use Adam Lovasz's phrase, before he too turns to Deleuze: Technically, the image could only be achieved by splicing two images, by filming the scene twice—once with the anchor present and again without him. He is ambiguous: both *here* and *not-here*, present and gone. Like a ghost.

This is like K's corpse, a vision that separates the subject from its body. This is also unlike K's corpse: Rather than showing us (threatening us with) what we ejected to become a subject, this image threatens us with never having become a subject, after we've ejected. And as if we never did. Like the Bacon portraits, the face is disrupted. Unlike those paintings, here, some of the face is entirely missing. A parody of our pandemic mask-wearing.

■

Animal Beta Project is a group of internet sleuths, *armchair detectives*, who specialize in identifying and reporting animal abuse assailants. They formed in direct response to "1 Boy 2 Kittens." They predicted and alerted authorities of the likelihood that this individual would kill. They accurately identified and located Magnotta long before the authorities did. They have subsequently identified and reported other creators—of a video of a dog being thrown off a roof in Egypt, a video bragging about and endorsing dog- and cockfighting, the videos "Dog Tornado" and "Cat Dryer." Most recently, they assisted in the arrest of the couple who created crush videos (stomp porn), Brent Justice and Ashley Richard, formerly of Waco, Texas.

When "1 Lunatic 1 Icepick" was uploaded, Magnotta was immediately recognized by the group. The *video guy* of Animal Beta Project, Alex DeLarge, suspected that the acts depicted were fake. Nonetheless, the group made it their obligation to identify Magnotta: *We have to determine if it's his face in the video.* Over the next two days, DeLarge locked himself in his office, video-conferencing with other members of the group, analyzing every individual frame of the video.

■

When school began again and the pandemic continued regardless, I refused to require my students to turn on their cameras for class. The scholarship and advice that was coming out at the time was divided: It seemed the younger the student, the more vociferous of an explanation that live, living visual presence would have a positive effect on learning; but there were many ways to facilitate that learning without the requirement, and there were ways to encourage that video to be turned on without the requirement, which, I thought, was the ideal.

I've watched a student get his hair done during class. Watched a student shop at the campus bookstore. From their laps, I have watched many students drive their cars—I can't tell where. So many meals have been eaten in front of me as I teach, full meals, dinner-table meals. I met a student's child, who sat and attended class with her every day, often distracting and interrupting her. We all loved to watch as a student's cat came up and sniffed the camera—the student always seated too far away to do anything about it very quickly, if at all. And I saw so many students in bed. Some were upright, but others slept, even after class had ended—their cameras still on, still sleeping, the onus on me to somehow protect their privacy, to end the meeting when they themselves couldn't leave it. A responsibility not to watch them, even though I could and even though they couldn't have stopped me.

I watched one student as he folded laundry. I appreciated so much that his camera was on that I couldn't bring myself to reprimand him for being shirtless. Doing laundry was his way of getting ready for class, like the frantic shuffling to get materials out of our backpacks upon arriving to class. Those brief glimpses of his naked torso were like seeing him in the hallway, aware that soon I'd be his teacher, but, for now, we are just passing. When he was shirtless again in class, and then again, upright in his bed, only face and shoulders visible, I still didn't reprimand him.

What, I wondered, is appropriate for a masculine-presenting student, anyway. I've seen just as much of my students in a physical pre-pandemic classroom: muscle shirts exposing the entire torso, depending on how he bends, and, now, our culture of gray sweatpants. (Your bulge, mine.) Was it inappropriate just to *infer* that he was shirtless, there underneath the frame of the camera, or did I need to confirm his shirtlessness, which I suppose I could only have done by asking if his nipples were exposed. *Are your nipples exposed. Can I see your nipples.* And maybe this is, in fact, about consent: *Are you trying to show me your nipples.* And what if they were covered by his sheets or a strapless top—is the illusion of shirtlessness as inappropriate. What is it about a nipple, anyway, that is so vulgar we should look away. And why does he have to wear a shirt in his own home—when I am not there and none of us are there and he lives alone and he likes to be shirtless all the time, and I would too if I looked like that, and, besides, no one is fucking paying attention in class anyway, not *to* class, because they don't give a shit about literature and are counting on their D's and F's to be turned into pandemic-specific emergency fails, which apparently don't affect their GPA or financial aid, and the ones who *do* pay attention are paying attention to me and my reactions to them, not to the shirtless student.

That glimpse of his nipples while he folded laundry, when he raised his arms to put his shirt on, was brief and, I think, accidental. So it was arousing: a glimpse of what I thought I shouldn't have seen, because he was seemingly unaware that I, we, could see. I was not turned on the same way when he was not folding laundry, when he just chose to be shirtless, just bare shoulders and chest, Schrödinger's nipples, unseen by the camera and both covered and uncovered.

■

I've always sought out evidence of the sexual, of the sexual lives of those around me, of those who I am sexual with, without me. When I house-sat as a kid, I'd rummage through drawers and laundry looking for condoms and cum stains. Years later, a boyfriend would share the porn he watched with me, and we'd watch it together. Then, while fucking me, my ex would grab my throat from behind and pull my chin up toward the porn on the television for me to watch—for him to watch me watch, aroused by my seeming arousal, when the truth is I was never really aroused at all.

He made me perform on cam, with and without him, and he made me have sex with others, with him. He made it so that my sex and sexuality were always on display for him. Evidence, then, was never really an issue until we stopped having sex and I stopped having sex but he didn't: the same rummaging for cum stains but more often looking for the porn he would watch without me and the guys he'd be fucking without me. Web browsing history. Shared computers. The same password for multiple accounts.

This was not jealousy. It did, however, always leave me feeling self-conscious—or jealous. This was sexual: When I would masturbate without him, I was masturbating to the idea of him masturbating to the porn I was watching that he had watched. Watching and imagining what it is that turns him on, at what point did he cum, and how close could I get to that. A desire for my eyes to be his, aroused by the idea that my body, in a temporal and maybe physical way, is or is at least mimicking his.

I thought this was about being watched, about watching being watched—about the physical confirmed by the digital. I thought that this was similar to my confusing *wanting to be* with *wanting to be with* someone. I was imagining being desired again, imagining seeing myself desired at all—whether that was in my body or in his.

■

Once, while he was at work, I pulled his laptop out from under the couch, noting its angle and orientation. I sat down with it on my lap, and when I opened it, fly already unzipped, it wasn't a log-in screen or desktop that greeted me but my own face. I watched it register a question before disbelief, then repulsion at seeing my own face seeing my own face on his computer through the webcam he had left recording the whole day so that he could listen to it later to see if I had been cheating on him.

I stopped its recording and skipped through the video, all black except the beginning and end: his face closing the laptop, my face opening. The video, the blackness, had no evidence of anything. I knew this. And I skipped through it anyway to see what he would have seen, to imagine my eyes as his own, leaning into that blackness to hear what he would hear. If there were no sounds in the recording, it would have meant that I was not home, which would have meant I was elsewhere, which would have meant I was cheating; if there were sounds of literally anything in the apartment, it would have sounded to him like fucking.

I couldn't bear it: The recording was the only thing that could prove I hadn't cheated on him, *but*. I couldn't bear it, knowing that I had been violated in this way. The recording was proof that he didn't trust me, and my face, there at the end, looking at me in disgust, was accusatory. I couldn't bear it, this evidence manufactured against me. I couldn't bear it, so I didn't. I deleted it. And this action was proof, to him, that there was something incriminating worth deleting, another justification for his violences.

■

I could give you his name to google (I won't), and if you were to look for images of him, you'd find only one—all the rest, scrubbed. You wouldn't find what I can find, like this picture where his eyes are caught in an offset blink—the one Pixar uses for veracity and others use to make characters look inebriated. He is, in fact, inebriated here, in this picture. He's drunk. He's seated on the floor beside his bed. His torso is naked, and he leans toward me, one arm outstretched and the other indecipherably between his legs, nipples hidden by arms and shadow although the tattoo of a web on his chest is visible. *Something sticky. Like it holds us together.* I want to know if he remembers this, if he knows what his own drunken hand was doing between his legs in this moment. I want to know if his performance had already ended or had only just begun.

We consolidate our identities: More veteran influencers laugh when newer ones have different handles for each platform. Success, for them, correlates to their addressability: being seen, being findable and found. Some use their actual names in and for their usernames; sometimes we use an alternate name for our virtual self while we remain true to our actual name in the waking world. He intentionally tries to obscure his identities by having a different username, a different legal name, a different alias for each website and platform. When you find one, it is difficult to find the others, but if you have already found the antecedent, his body, the actual person, all these disparate identities contract back onto it without difficulty.

■

There are websites, all identical in function, that generate GIFS, videos, and thumbnails, like this, of him and what I imagine to be thousands of other Chaturbate performers. I assume these are recorded anonymously, by nobody, a bot—auto-clickers opening room after room and recording all at once and indiscriminately. Even if they stop performing, delete the account—even once he stopped performing and deleted his account, I could find him. All you need to do is google the name (a name) with CHATURBATE and, maybe, click REPEAT THE SEARCH WITH OMITTED RESULTS INCLUDED.

In my search for him, I click to include those results, and out floods new, unrelated content. From eight results to seven million, supposedly *too similar*: *The Atlantic*, *GQ*, JSTOR, a pdf of Aesop's Fables, an article from the New York Public Library. These had separately matching search terms and partial matches, but none of them were actually similar to the initial eight.

Once Google delivers us to the image, though, we are generally directed to purchase access to the media. For a more popular (addressable, desirable) performer, these are quickly distributed through more mainstream avenues: MyVidster, XTube, PornHub, Telegram. His never surfaced, though, either for being too unpopular or for his performing too infrequently.

I paid the money for the files, and there was only that one, single image: his drunk-blinking and a mostly dark and mostly nondescript bedroom.

The image is not explicit, but it is erotic both for the Schrödinger's masturbation and its being taken (distributed) without consent. It is erotic because it is a picture of my ex-husband, of my violent ex-husband. Erotic because I can find it even though I shouldn't be able to. Because I shouldn't *want* to find it, but I do. Because my body should protect itself from reacting this way. But it doesn't, and it continues to do so. Because I have manufactured such a great distance between our antecedents and then, all of a sudden, here he is, *reconstituted through technology*.

Yes, and. That thing I still won't say. Repeating and working through.

■

He strangled me two days before Thanksgiving, and I told him to be moved out before January. I returned to Chicago from a long holiday with family to find, much to my surprise, that he had. The abuse continued in various forms regardless.

When I answered the front-door buzzer to the apartment, already dark outside, cold because winter and because dark and because Chicago, I heard crying. He was crying, drunk, I could tell by how vociferous. All I could say was *no*, immediately aware that at any moment, another resident would not only recognize him but also let him into the building, thinking he still lived there. I couldn't stand the thought of him banging at my door, of being trapped in what was once our apartment, now with the person-sized hole in the bedroom door, the broken coffeepot, and my back always against that fridge. So I didn't. I left quickly out the back of the building and into the shallow snow.

The sparrows that dive for bugs between pedestrians at the beach were gone, and the people there were fewer than during the day, even in winter. But the beach was both public and well-lit.

Eventually, I circled back, widely, to the apartment building, looking and listening for him. I couldn't hear his cries, but I could see, in the distance, there he was, crying on the curb outside my home. He fumbled to get up and harass a passerby. I left again, went further this time, and returned, shivering and tired, spying on my own apartment from behind a bush, wondering if I'd be seen looking and considered to be the creep, the threat preventing someone from going home.

That I couldn't see him, though, didn't mean he wasn't there. So I opened Scruff. This is a trick that relies upon our inability or unwillingness to log off or sign out, our phones constantly pinging and tracking—so, we, always trackable.

The grid was the same as always—me, then the five who never change, the neighbors you never fuck so as not to shit where you eat. I was frozen, unable to decide whether he was here or not here, until I scrolled further and saw him at the usual distance, far enough away to almost disappear in the technology. Left unblocked for this very reason.

■

Between his homophobic microaggressions and conservative commentary on Magnotta's sexuality, Whitney carves out the space in his book to also disparage millennials. He gives the same explanation of social media use as what Anna Delvey's attorney supposedly used in his closing statement: We all have this side of us. Magnotta *exaggerated and embellished* his life and identity: *Many of us attempt to use the Internet constantly to make ourselves look better. If you don't think I am correct go check out Instagram. Look how hot I am, look how popular I am, look at all the friends I have, look at how much fun I am having, look at how perfect my ass is. In today's social media world, vanity is often thought of as a virtue.*

We post that which aligns with how we wish to be viewed, he is right. But I don't think it is *vanity*, and I certainly don't think this means vanity is perceived as a *virtue*.

These are all externally marked qualities: *fun* by what we are seen doing, *popular* by who and how many we are seen with, *hot* by our bodies relative to others'. While we can *claim* to be any of this as often and ardently as we want, these qualities are also externally *affirmed* by likes and follows and collabs, none of which we can get until we already are hot popular fun. We have to be seen being seen before anyone takes notice. All these qualities, a matter of addressability. Never who we are but rather what we share.

I share, therefore I am.

■

At 11:06 a.m. on August 9th, 2016, the Circuit Court of Cook County granted me an order of protection from the man who is now my ex-husband.

This order protected my home and my work and prohibited any *telephone calls, mail, emails, faxes, written notes, or communication through third parties* for two years. This order was granted to keep him from committing

PHYSICAL ABUSE

HARASSMENT

INTERFERENCE WITH PERSONAL LIBERTY

STALKING

of or against me and any other protected person. I wanted him ordered to undergo counseling. *At TBD for a duration of TBD.* The judge did not grant this, resulting in a pen scribble across two lines of printed text. I told the attorney appointed to my case by the Domestic Violence Legal Clinic that if he were to retaliate, lash out, hurt me, it would be through my dog. For the duration of the order, I was granted *exclusive care, custody or control* of *dog "Sylvia" greyhound (8 yr. old) (brindle colored).*

There are so many empty checkboxes. One indicates that he was not ordered *to stay away [or] to refrain from taking, transferring, encumbering, concealing, harming, or otherwise disposing of the animal.* Others suggest that he was not prohibited from intimidating or exploiting me, not that he'd have been able to, given the remainder of the order; not that he'd have wanted to, given the penalty:

ANY KNOWING VIOLATION MAY RESULT IN A FINE OR IMPRISONMENT.

STALKING IS A FELONY.

He didn't come around the apartment building anymore, but I wasn't being protected. Such orders only protect in that they threaten to punish; they do not prevent. Even still, none of the violations I reported were acted upon by the attorneys or the court.

Not when I received messages from his best friend's Facebook account about him, saying what my ex wanted to say to me, for him. Not when that same account sent messages to my mother, someone who is not protected but who would convey the message nonetheless. *Communication through third parties.*

They didn't do anything when that same account messaged yet again, claiming to be the person from whom I'm protected, even though I already knew that it really was him, and they didn't do anything about the times he messaged me on other apps. Either these don't count as *emails* or a person cannot be punished for written messages or I could only ever have been protected from a single version of him that existed, apparently, behind only one, singular account. Which account that was, they could never have known. These courts and attorneys do not have time or know-how to deal in IP addresses and location tracking. They are right, though: Anyone could have said or done or coerced me to do anything, and I would not have been protected—they would not have been punished—because anyone can pretend to be anyone else on the internet.

It sounds dramatic, I know, and much like an unfounded technophobia, a *To Catch a Predator* era oversimplification, the same as the anti–online dating rhetoric of *You can't really know who these people are* I heard so much of when we all started dating online.

Of course, now we know, we do—we know how easy it is to be exactly someone else.

■

Magnotta created hundreds of profiles and accounts across social media to post and comment on posts, to post about himself as if a fan or stalker, triangulating and humiliating himself into existence:

HE IS IN FACT NOW LIVING IN THE CARIBBEAN WITH HIS NEW WIFE KARLA HOMOLKA.
MAN IS THAT LUKA MAGNOTTA SO FUCKED UP OR WHAT?
THERE IS APPARENTLY A VIDEO CIRCULATING AROUND THE DEEP WEB CALLED ONE LUNATIC ONE ICE PICK VIDEO. DOES ANYONE HAVE A COPY OF IT?

These facades, these personae are not entirely unlike Robert Phillips' *conditional identity*, described in his definition of abjection: Like our more traditional social markers, when we are stripped of digital alter egos, we are all these mutable, formless objects. Identity, a queer artifact; social media, a queering enterprise.

■

I use my own conditional identity, now, to search Scruff for him, nine hundred miles away. I only need to know an estimated location and I can sort from there. I can guess usernames. When I sit, tap, open Scruff, I meet his gaze there in the top left corner, my own avatar. His name is my name in this virtual grid.

Desirable, albeit in someone else's body.

■

Lines 5–10 and 12–16 of the order are all blank, literally devoid of meaning. Then, 17: *Respondent is further ordered and/or enjoined as follows.* There, on these once-empty lines, the typed words of the attorney:

THE RESPONDENT SHALL NOT DISTRIBUTE, POST ON ANY WEBSITES OR SOCIAL MEDIA, OR OTHERWISE DISSEMINATE REVEALING PICTURES AND/OR VIDEOS OF THE PETITIONER.

Revenge porn had been around for so long, and the internet made its dissemination so much easier, its number of both participants and viewers more numerous. In 2014 and 2015 the nation saw numerous criminal lawsuits against *cyber exploitation* and extortion. My attorney had taken notice.

I had forgotten this particular protection, but now I recall the attorney's pastel periwinkle shirt, the frosted glass walls, my own shrinking, shrunk comportment. My only concern at the time was immediate and local, for Sylvia; but his concern extended beyond the physical person and possessions and into another reality in which I also existed, vulnerable to such offenses.

■

If bots have been doing this for a decade (have they), then the times he made us perform on cam together—because he needed the money and was bored with our sex anyway and we didn't have enough of either—could also have been recorded, turned to GIFs and thumbnails, available to anyone who knows the account name, the identity, our fake identities, and the name of the site we used.

How strange, to contract a person into being.

The person on cam, the person I was on cam—who I claimed to be, who I was forced to be, paid and beaten to be—is long since forgotten. I can recall the website, the alias, the account setup and age verification, which was an arduous project then of printing documents and photographing them and emailing them to myself (and they're still there, in the archive of my email), but I don't remember the username. It would be humiliating to be discovered in this way, to contract that person there, then, back to me here and now. Luckily, there is nothing that links us. That version of me no longer has an antecedent. There's only everything after. And everything before.

I imagine that my violated body *does* exist somewhere in an image taken by a bot years ago, but its discovery would be by pure chance: No one is sorting and sifting through these archival websites with all this stored data, one by one, username by username, looking for *me*. No one who does go through the data, one by one, username by username, would know if they saw me. No one is clicking on SHOW OMITTED RESULTS to find me. I try this myself, and I'm really fucking good at googling, and I do not find these files that may or may not exist.

Google, of course, indexing only one internet.

■

There's a video circulating the internet news, the kind that's fashionable enough for social media but rarely does more than paraphrase a research article's title and, maybe, its abstract. It's of a sea slug's head moving independently of its body—the head, now its own entire body, the entire slug itself, crawling over and rasping the dark green leaf that was once its body but is no longer. In proper internet fashion, the titles are misleading:

MEET THE SEA SLUGS THAT CHOP OFF THEIR OWN HEAD
THIS SEA SLUG CUT OFF ITS OWN HEAD
SEA SLUG DECAPITATES ITSELF

But there is no chopping, no cutting, no decapitation in this singular video, common to all 8,140 of Google's results matching the search term SLUG DECAPITATE: The video is so segmented, so abbreviated that the slug is always already headless. But I care less for results than the process.

Show, don't tell.

The closest analog I can think of, appropriate or otherwise, is that a lizard can snap off its own tail. I want to see it, that process. I want to know what it looks like when cells divide and disconnect, eject, reject each other, what it looks like for flesh to tear itself asunder, to strangle itself to a pinch and fall off. I want to see if I can see, exactly, what is happening in this miraculous moment.

■

I sit at my desk and watch videos. I watch a dozen of just-tails flopping and writhing and violently shaking to find a video in which the lizard has a tail at the start and does not have a tail by the end. The young shirtless boy shows his father, behind the camera, what he found. I see the dark head poking out from the *okay* of his thumb and index finger, and he grabs it from behind, by the tail, and holds it up for his father to record. Barely a moment of the boy's delight, and then it drops. His voice is unafraid and apparently unsurprised. Just the observation: *Its tail fell off.* I am impressed by this young boy's composure as the tail convulses in his fingers and, a second later, in his palm; and I am unnerved by the way dismemberment has become everyday.

Suddenly, *Oh, I know what happened.* Then, more excitedly, *I know what happened.* This is one of those facts we all learn at that age and are captivated by, the unimportant kind, specific and uncanny—the same kind that I find increasingly spurious with age and lack of experiential evidence. Echidnas have a poisonous spur. Cut the flesh from a snake bite and suck out the venom. Pee on a jellyfish sting. We'd float in lava. Stop drop and roll. Cows have four stomachs, and birds have a separate organ for ingested stones. This is analogous to our appendix. A beaver's raspberry-flavored anus. Strawberries aren't berries, but watermelons are. Don't eat the seeds. Tornadoes can tear everything out of the kitchen cabinets and drawers while leaving everything else undamaged (here is a picture), and it will pass you over if you are fetal in a ditch. You can wrap the equator with your veins. Twice. A sniper bullet is faster than sound, so you'll be dead before you hear the shot. We remain conscious for several seconds after decapitation, sometimes can even speak, blink (Anne Boleyn).

■

Google's results are pulled and ordered according to meaning, relevance, quality, usability, and context. This means, for example, that it will prioritize sites that are cited by (hyperlinked to) others that contain the search terms or their synonyms. This means that certain iterations of the video, with similarly meaning but unaffected titles, appear pages deep in Google results:

SOME SEA SLUGS GROW NEW BODIES
SEA SLUG'S DETACHED HEAD CAN CRAWL
SEA SLUG SHOWS EXTREME CASE OF REGENERATION

These appear less relevant to Google because of the language, the word choice, but they are in fact closer to the original source. This is of no import to Google; instead, only the number of times a site is linked matters. It is easy, then, to interpret popularity and salability as being other criteria, albeit unstated.

These less popular iterations omit the very words that draw our attention to the others. The search results demonstrate our interest is in decapitation, chopping off, cutting off. We have admitted ourselves to our search engines. Our browsing histories, our YouTube wormholes, and our *explore* feed all align to prove that we are not only the type to seek the things we don't or can't or shouldn't experience in our lives, the violent and taboo, the extreme, but also the type to be always tempted by something incrementally *more*.

■

My initial thought was that animals, like these slugs, are *decapitated* while people are *beheaded*. Testing this out, my partner reminds me that Charlie in Ari Aster's *Hereditary* is *decapitated* rather than *beheaded*: She goes into anaphylactic shock at a party and her brother, Peter, drives her to the hospital. She gasps and pants in the backseat, unable to breathe, she can't breathe. *I can't breathe*. She rolls down the window and hangs her head out, desperate for air. Peter swerves to avoid a large dead animal in the road, and Charlie's head is taken off by a telephone pole.

We intuit that a beheading is punitive, and dictionaries all make it clear that a *beheading* is a decapitation. Asking Google (how many times, in how many different ways) reveals that most people believe these words *mean the same*, but they do not come to a consensus on why *behead* and *decapitate* are not interchangeable.

I dig and read and translate, I ask my partner more, I email my Old English professor. *Why do we know the difference if dictionaries don't tell us the difference.* I learn the etymologies: *behealdian* and *decapitate*. The roots, *heafod* and *cap*, are identical, the one's shift through Germanic languages, predictable; no differences in meaning between *be-/-ian* and *de-/-ate*. The difference is not in word meaning or in connotation but maybe somewhere in diatype—the field of use, the mode, the tenor: If I am a queen and you are my subject, I will perform a beheading (not a decapitation) because I want this performance to be about my authority over you; if I ask about how a decapitation is performed, maybe I'll learn something about the guillotine or slugs, but I am clearly asking someone like a scientist.

The most fascinating part of all this, though, is how *behead* doubles on itself: A person who is *beheaded* also always already has been. Both a state of being and its own verb. This is how the word elides the fact of action: There has been a cut, a slice, a *decapitation*, but that's not what we're discussing. Always result, never process. Always able to tell but never to show.

■

I've searched for decapitation before, for the action, the cut, the mechanics. At the time, I thought it'd be illegal, it'd be banned, it'd be in another language. I thought, then, that *our* internet would not allow us to get to *their* internet. I believed that it could not and should not be found.

The curiosity came from suspicion: It might not even be real. This was a disbelief likely informed by recent hoax-like horror. Three years before, *The Blair Witch Project* was released, and for a full year before that, we were inundated with police reports and missing persons posters littered over dozens of websites, which suggested its veracity. But then the most horrible thing we've ever seen turned out to be fake. So, when I searched for this thing that could not possibly be found and I found it, I had the opportunity to prove it was not real by watching it. If I could find it, it had to be fake or just a pre-cut clip, the SLUG DECAPITATES ITSELF version.

So now, again: Can I find it. *It*, because it seemed a singular thing then:

BEHEADING VIDEO

Today the search yields more than seventy-one million results (almost double what was found just a year ago), which has as much to do with diffusion and duplication as it does with frequency and occurrence, with our ancient and continued *obsession with the head as symbol of the thinking living being*, with more people online and writing online and referencing older online people writing. This number of results is both cause and effect of how these videos are now quotidian.

Oxford anthropologist Frances Larson's TED Talk, "Why Public Beheadings Get Millions of Views," does not account for my own curiosity or desire to myth-bust. Instead, she looks out at the crowd and speaks in the plural, for everyone in the room, including herself: *We think a beheading is nothing to do with us, even as we click on the screen to watch.*

These videos are *a twenty-first-century event*, she tells us, looking up at seemingly even the most distant audience member, *that takes place in our living rooms, at our desks, on our computer screens*. She explains that the action, the crime, the death is *stretched out in time and place*. This is (or is an effect of) what we call *liveness*, a phenomenon we saw with the television, just over half a century earlier. Barthes calls it a *temporal hallucination: false on the level of perception, true on the level of time.* It is not here, and it has indeed been somewhere. A paradox. Here *and* not-here.

The action, the crime, the death, Larson suggests, is stretched. Then so too must be the actors, the victims and the terrorists—*entities with visible form but without material substance.* The line between *being* and *not-being*, between being here and there, somewhere and nowhere, erased.

Lots of people watch. She says an estimated 1.2 million in Britain watched the beheading of James Foley in just days after its release. She estimates—and it is always an estimation with the internet, with illicit material, with self-reporting, isn't it—23 percent of Americans had watched, and 9 percent to the end (a calculation that is simultaneously a judgment).

Every one of the blue-lighted audience members looks somehow attentive while refusing interest or, god forbid, excitement. They watch her without averting their gaze, but there is a general shrinking: shoulders slumped, heads low, many hands at the mouth and nobody smiling. She addresses this blue cloud of shame fallen over the audience: She observes that we like to believe that *the things we do online are somehow less real* and, thus, *watching is a passive activity*—but it's not.

■

The first result used to be Wikipedia. It only recently dropped in popularity, now tucked between Zelenskyy's comments on an apparent Russian beheading of a Ukrainian soldier and, underneath, the woman who reportedly birthed a decapitated baby.

The Wikipedia article is part of their series on Jihadism, a hyperlinked list with names and dates, brief descriptions sometimes, separated by years as headings:

2002

2004

2014

2015

2016

2017

2018

2019

2021

2022

2023

It doesn't seem like 2020 is going to be added. (There's a joke, here, about social distancing and Zoom-bombing, I am sure.) But I am drawn to this suspiciously extensive range:

2005–2013

In her 2015 Talk, Larson lists only seven individuals beheaded by the Islamic State. *Their names have become familiar: James Foley, Steven Sotloff, David Haines, Alan Henning, Peter Kassig, Haruna Yukawa, Kenji Goto Jogo*, all their photos on the screen behind her. I see these same names in Wikipedia, and between the most recent she mentions, Kenji Goto, and the date of her talk, there were public videos of the beheading of forty-nine Egyptian and Ethiopian Christians. Between the deaths of Peter Kassig and Haruna Yukawa, eighteen Syrian soldiers were beheaded.

Larson is not concerned, in her present moment, with the beheading of Nick Berg, which in 2004 became one of the most watched videos, perhaps the first truly viral video to exist. Its unprecedented number of views shut down the hosting website, al-ansar.biz, unable to handle the server traffic.

She is also not concerned with the rest of those beheaded the same year as Berg: Paul Marshall Johnson, Kim Sun-il, Georgi Lazov, Mohammed Mutawalli, Eugene Armstrong, Jack Hensley, Kenneth Bigley, Shosei

Koda. Unmentioned are the firsts of internet beheadings, two from the late nineties during the conflicts in Chechnya and Afghanistan. Meanwhile, even Wikipedia has forgotten the names of Margaret Hassan, Dumrus Kumdereli, Ali Hussein Jassem Mohammad al-Zubaidi, Ahmad Alwan Hussein al-Mahmadawi, Yevgeny Aleksandrovich Rodionov, Salakhetdin Azizov, Ghulam Nabi, and Muath al-Kasasbeh.

I don't know if there are Q&A sessions after TED Talks, but, were I there, I'd consider asking about the sixty-seven rhetorically absent, missing, beheaded, and why we are instead familiar with only these seven. But I wouldn't because my desire to account for so many decapitations might seem too eager. Because the desire *to account for* may be misunderstood as a desire *to watch*, or, apparently worse, *watch to the end*. Because the question I have is less to do with her answer than with my accusations—toward myself and her.

■

We should stop watching.

Larson's plural is complex. Semantically, *we* is herself and her audience. Rhetorically, *we* refers to the 9 percent, the 23 percent who have watched, whether or not we are in the audience. Rhetorically, then, *we* have *all* watched. Except when she says this, it isn't the voice of an ego who has watched.

The forbidding, the *should stop*: An ego can't but relate to objects as they are. That is, even when she tries to sound more empathetic, appear more vulnerable, be personable, be part of *we*, her message is that of our superego, judging both it and us.

K: *To each ego its object; to each superego its abject.*

Larson claims that watching perpetuates not only the humiliation and suffering of the victims but also the desire of the terrorists. Hers seems to be an outrage that, when and because we watch, they win. (*We* lose.) When we watch, their message is not only heard but also disseminated.

The videos are propagandist. In *Killing for Culture: From Edison to Isis*, David Kerekes and David Slater suggest the purpose of these videos is threefold: to terrorize, of course, to recruit support, and to encourage imitative acts. In contrast, Mexican drug cartel videos are uploaded to YouTube (and subsequently removed) for two reasons: territory and honor. These videos are significantly crueler and more barbarous, death never the end and never quite the start either: Rival gang members suffer protracted torture before their deaths by, say, beheading, and are further humiliated, their bodies subject to ignominy in a series of one-upping and retaliation.

■

No real attention was ever given to the videos of Syrians and Iraqis being killed en masse. The beheading of James Foley, this single individual, was so offensive that British Prime Minister David Cameron canceled the rest of his vacation and returned to work. The police announced that it would be a crime to view, distribute, and link to the video. *Potentially.* They weren't actually sure of what the offense would be. Meanwhile, Prime Minister Cameron locked himself up in his office to watch the video, to analyze it frame by frame to discover the killer.

■

It is easy for me to simply say that Larson is wrong, that there is no decapitation at my desk, in my home—that we delude ourselves when we call these *live* beheadings. Such videos, all videos, all referential and representational media, are only indices of *it has indeed already happened*. Some things simply cannot happen *again*, at my desk or elsewhere. As if someone could be beheaded twice. Or 1.4 million times. The images of the sword the knife the head the dry cheeks the slack jaw the wagging tongue are only images on our screens. Our perception, that we think we see it happening again, happening now, is false. The problem: False perception is still perception, and a delusion is exactly as real as anything else that is *perceived.*

The video of Daniel Pearl's beheading, as it exists, does not show his beheading but, rather, a reenactment with his already-beheaded corpse—a fact that never mattered to the media or any of those who believed they had just seen a *live* beheading.

In 2004 Benjamin Vanderford released footage on a militant website of his own beheading. Seated in a lawn chair, rocking back and forth, no telltale orange jumpsuit, the murderer armed only with only a kitchen knife and bad acting. Like the Jihadi beheading videos, it was political in nature: The creator intended to demonstrate the hypocrisy of our news media, the ability for misinformation to spread. The video was convincing enough that it was temporarily hosted by and accredited to the Islamic Global Media Center right up until the FBI knocked on Vanderford's door. The event was spectacle, the press coverage sensational, widely reported and distributed, albeit months after its release, as real.

On the internet, there is no difference between fantasy and reality.

■

Junco and Michi's boss at Sunny Plant Sales hasn't come in to work. *Michi, what do you think's going on. Why's everyone disappearing.* Instead of answering, Michi calls around in search of him.

The film itself only offers three possibilities, and not for the *why*, but only the *how*. The first is suicide, like Taguchi's. The second is disintegration—becoming ash and staying there, wherever you've been, now a stain on the wall and floor. In the case of Taguchi, these are not mutually exclusive: When Yabe goes to Taguchi's apartment, he sees the black smudge where we had previously seen his body hang. (Then Yabe looks again and sees Taguchi standing in front of that smudge before he disappears again.) The third is disappearance.

As if with a sudden inspiration, Junco says, *I'll go look for him.* She rushes out of her rooftop workplace, leaving Michi to answer the ringing phone.

Boss.

Tasukete.

Yabe. Are you Yabe.

Somewhere else, lower in that smooth, gray building, Junco removes red duct tape from around the seal of a door. She opens it and enters the dark room.

While running after Junco, Michi stops at the sight of this opened, unsealed door, red duct tape still holding cardboard up over the window. She enters and finds Junco frightened and crawling away from her friend's attempted consolation. As Junco is pulled to her feet, they both see the ghost who was already so near them, so still. Michi makes to get her friend out of the room, but she stays. It looks like she wants to stay, looks like she pushes Michi so that she could have just another moment in the room with this ghost, hypnotized by and drawn to it, but so afraid. Only as the ghost draws nearer to them with its arms up can Michi finally pull Junco away.

The ghost's approach was alarming, yes—this pose we think is meant to make us appear larger, like we are supposed to do to ward off a bear—but how it manifested was so calm and still that Junco didn't even notice the presence, crawling right up underneath it. The ghost stands looming over Junco with its arms raised, hair flowing ethereally.

Junco freezes and she watches it watch her, frozen. In these long five seconds, Junco could be grabbed, swallowed, touched, hurt.

When the film cuts to a shot from down the hallway, now seeing these two run toward us, the camera, and away from the ghost, we can still see her visible in the background, covering her face in her hands, forlorn—a pose we've come to associate with Miss Havishams and widows overlooking the sea. The ghost is dejected, mourning this connection. Abject.

■

Once, during a fight, I locked myself and our dog in the bedroom or, rather, locked my ex out of it. When he left the apartment, it was always disconcerting because I never knew when he'd return: He could be smoking, he could have gone to the bar. At the bar, he'd usually get blackout drunk. He'd often do drugs (*I must have been roofied*). He could have been taken home by someone from that basement, the trough. He could return in five minutes or tomorrow afternoon.

When he returned, he literally broke through that locked door. Kicked and punched his way through, splintered it open with a torso-sized hole. It was so easy. And it could have been even more dramatic if that door wasn't already hollow, the cheap kind that cheap apartments put up—certainly bought in bulk, functional for privacy but not for safety. Profit at the cost of—what.

I left the bedroom through the door. I unlocked and opened it. His rage and accusations, his frenetic illogic, his volume and the total amount of physical and emotional space he occupied in that apartment made me shake as I walked away from him. I made it only as far as the next room, the kitchen, when he strangled me, my back to the fridge.

■

The victims in these videos all seem docile and calm. People speculate that this is because, since the videos were important propaganda, the event was frequently rehearsed, right up to the final cut. As the final take was being filmed, the victims would have thought this was yet another rehearsal. Right up to the cut.

Hickey, Petschi, Kennedy, and Shaw, along with, I'm sure, countless and unnamed others, were forced to watch beheading videos before they themselves were decapitated.

■

The outrage at not shutting our eyes seems to have very little to do, as Larson suggests, with the message of the videos. We, *we*, are capable of closure, of filling in any gap, completing any image, following patterns, by making conclusions about what comes next. As the films *The Kingdom* and *Body of Lies* demonstrate, all we need to see is a small room containing a camcorder on a tripod, tarps on the floor, tarps on the walls, maybe a blade, maybe someone bound. Throw in some Arabic and lo-fi image quality, and we (think we) know. Even a thumbnail holds *the message* Larson discusses, because we have already manufactured the message within ourselves: We do not *need* to see the video through to the end to know what happens.

That is, the message is not found exclusively in the content; the message is overwhelmingly in the context—that same context that makes only seven names familiar, the same context that encourages us to see death, these deaths, on the news, that tells us that there are things we should not see on the internet but that are readily available nonetheless. This pre–content warning context of a general *the footage you are about to see*.

Larson suggests that the terrorists' point, their desired outcome, their message is lost if we don't watch. The problem: Their message has apparently *not* been lost despite 77 percent, 91 percent of us never having seen the decapitation. That is, the fact that *many of us watch* does not capture just how many do not.

What Larson's Talk makes very clear is that it isn't just the terrorists who can benefit from our watching. As she sympathizes with our shame and shaming, it becomes clear that we (Larson and her audience) have as great an ideological need to watch the videos as the terrorists have to make them: Our watching perpetuates our own ideology, our own message and the possibility of advancing our notions of superiority, modernity, enlightenment—with all the inherent imperialism of that word. Our consumption of these videos manifests an enemy, stokes our xenophobia, and gives us our heathens:

We don't do that, Larson says. *It's barbaric.*

■

A willingness to shoot is a requirement of being a police officer. During training, we are meant to lose that inhibition, one that supposedly comes from our (unchecked) assumption that those we encounter have values similar to our own. *I'm not here to hurt them, so they won't hurt me.* Once we are trained, we no longer assume good in anyone. As if we are looking through RoboCop's visor, all people become *good* or *bad*, threat or not-threat.

The comments on the police training videos, like the one depicting the death of Deputy Kyle Dinkheller, were, before removal or deletion, rarely anything more than signs of solidarity, people barking out their academies and stations, announcing themselves to themselves. Quite often, though, by uniting under their *goodness*, their *brotherhood*, they identify exactly who and what they oppose. On MrMikesMondoVideo's upload of Constable Darrell Lunsford's death, the uploader's own comment, RACIAL SLURS WILL NOT BE TOLERATED, an index of the very thing being prohibited, alongside these and similar comments:

I COULD HEAR THEM SPEAKING SPANISH

MEXICANS

TRUMP 2020

JUST SOME BAD PEOPLE, LOOK AT WHAT HAPPENED AT THE TWIN TOWERS

■

Shock sites, these presumed pervert habitats, are at least *outwardly* dedicated to their promise of unbiased, uncensored news. In 2002 the FBI threatened Ted Hickman, owner of the company hosting Ogrish.com, with charges of obscenity, responding to the *heartless decision* to upload the video of Daniel Pearl's beheading—the one that doesn't actually show any decapitation. The video, however, was restored after the American Civil Liberties Union determined this was both a violation of the First Amendment and an illegitimate claim regardless: The 1996 federal obscenity law apparently applies only to sexual material.

Which is to say: Maybe we *should* stop watching. And maybe that's not the point.

■

But I told him that I like horror, that I don't scare easily. I said to him, *Have you seen this J-horror film*. He said, *Have you heard of. Do you know kevin.666, do you know BestGore.* I hadn't, and he showed me. On my computer, my search history. I didn't balk. He was so familiar with the site that he could recall usernames and video titles. He pulled up one, one that he *liked* or *enjoyed* or that *fascinated* him—I don't know why *this* one, but this one was special to him for some reason: a supposed escape artist, her legs bound in the air, her arms wrapped around her legs, hands cuffed behind, her torso submerged in water. She didn't escape. And the video continued to record regardless. And that's how I discovered that drowned bodies thrash, and that it takes so fucking long to suffocate.

I said, *You know what, I have a secret.* He was the first I had ever told: *Once, in college, just to see if I could.*

■

Junco's encounter with the ghost, with this *impossible object, non-body*, this *visible* yet *immaterial* thing leaves her petrified. While seated on the floor, Junco reaches for a blanket from off the bed and tucks it into her fetal body. She asks for help:

Tasukete. Tasukete. Tasukete.

■

If that mythical mirror were blurry or cracked, our united self, our *subject* would have become blurry or cracked too. In a Bacon portrait, there's nothing proper to project inward; its ambiguity, however, keeps us from outright rejecting it too.

(Fleischmann: *It was impossible to see myself, not because of what I was looking at, but rather because I couldn't get beyond what everyone else was looking at.*)

■

So Michi visits a convenience store for items to tend to a practically comatose Junco. As she walks with her items under her arm and in her hands, from one aisle to the next, our eye is drawn to a closing door, just past her head, in the otherwise empty store—the otherwise (suddenly) empty city. The next cut moves us to the as-yet-unseen person in the room behind the counter. Through their eyes—we know, because we are moving from the left, the door, to the right, where we will be seen in just a moment—we see Michi approach the counter and call for assistance. This overlap of sight is *hybrid subjectivity*: It's *me* Michi can't see.

The camera now positioned behind Michi, we can see the figure in a red work apron, standing still, face half-covered by some stainless-steel kitchen machinery, silent and unmoving. Cut to Michi's face, and there is a barely noticeable but unmistakable inhale and eye widening as her face shifts and twists to horror. Then (hybrid with Michi), we see the convenience store employee, still standing, still silent and unmoving, still only half visible from behind the machinery. Except now blurry, distorted, melting, as if smoke had filled the room or water slowly dripped down the glass between them. Indistinct.

Michi runs because what she has just witnessed cannot be assimilated, is *unthinkable*—unbearably *between* the possible and impossible. The window between, the employee's identity, their physical body—it is all fragile and shifting and melting, malleable.

■

That email to Clutch will never be sent, not because I don't want the feedback but because all it says is, *Interpolate me.* It has nothing at all to do with them, nothing that would require their individual person—nothing, in fact, that technically requires a person to begin with. Just that I perceive that reflection, that gaze, my own image in their sclera.

(You) give me your (my own) queer blessing.

It's nothing at all to do with *me* either. It's just pronouns and subjectivity, addressability and availability—here and not-here.

■

Michi was able to escape rattled but not ruined. Junco, however, having encountered this very real and unthinkable abjection, is gripped by an undoing that will not dissipate until she is properly and finally undone and she has lost her sense of self.

She does: She disintegrates into an ash that fills the air and disperses itself out the window.

This is what it means to lose our subjectivity. That's why everyone's disappearing from the city. Ironically, the only obvious sign that life carries on is a shop television turned to the news, a broadcast that continuously cycles through the photos and names of residents missing from Tokyo, Kanagawa, and Saitama.

II

THAT ORIGINAL STATE, "I" AM WEAK.

—JULIA KRISTEVA

Perhaps when I call my mother next, I will tell her that it's not that we are living bodies and the corpse is a dead body but, rather, that our living bodies emanate and the corpse does not, that a corpse is *a body without a soul.* Do your snakes make your soul leave your body. Now imagine your soul leaves, but your senses are still unsustainably operating in the body, still living. A husk, a *not-me*, not anymore. The corpse reminds you of all the snakes you had to throw up to become *only-me, just-me.*

There. That.

■

My family had a computer when I was growing up. It was a DOS, the kind of computer that ran entirely like a command prompt—the startup eventually yielding that gray-on-black screen, doing nothing until we'd respond to its C:\> and blinking underscore.

I'd insert a floppy disk, the 8" or 5.25", I can't remember which—my own hands so much smaller then—but they were actually floppy, unlike the more familiar 3.5", and I'd play games—*Tank Wars, Where in the World Is Carmen Sandiego* and the easier *Where in the USA Is Carmen Sandiego.* I was so young, that was all I could do—look through each and every letter on the keyboard until I found the one I wanted to guess in *Wheel of Fortune*, prompting the 8-bit yellow-skinned, green-dressed Vanna to shuffle over.

Later, after all my computer classes, after my father left, after my sister married, we got a new computer, one that could access the internet.

Yes, I listened to the handshake of the dial-up modem every time, and we coordinated internet use with expected phone calls. (See how we had to close one type of communication to open another.) I did all the things that we were doing on the internet then: not AOL but MSN Messenger until 3:00 a.m., asked Jeeves about anything and everything (*am I gay*), entered chatrooms, found porn (*am I gay*). *Sit, masturbate.*

It was a time before surfeit, a time when *favorite* did not refer to a corpus of an individual's *content* but rather a single image—because I had to wait for that long vertical image with a blue background of A GAY SAME ETHNICITY AS KEANU REEVES to load, line by line, hair, face, neck, and by then I may have finished.

Thumbnails, suggestion—always enough.

■

Even from a young age, my mother talked to us about death. Maybe because our yard is the resting place of fifty years' worth of pets. Maybe because she was wrecked by her own mother's sudden passing (*why would she call her daughter before calling the ambulance*). She was very intentional, I think, in her parenting: She made exactly two things absolutely known to the three of us, decades of repeating the same words so they stick. First: *Be all that you can be, but don't join the army*. Second: *Your body is just a vehicle.*

My mother is no *corpse fancier*, but we talk about death and dying regularly. My siblings laugh. When we talked most recently, she told me that, even though they are long passed, her parents are regularly in her dreams. My grandmother died at sixty-two, before I was old enough to remember her, get to know her, although there is a home movie of us: I can walk, and maybe I can talk (sort of), and I go to pet their cat, Sally. She tells me not to, because Sally'll *get me* or *scratch me* or something. Gramps died much more recently, in the apartment we built attached to my mom's house.

(A long time ago in Chicago, I woke up crying and had to immediately call my mother: *I need to know if Grandma would have liked me. I just have to know. I need to know if we would have been friends.* She said, *Oh, she would have loved you.*)

This most recent phone call, my mom talks about death in a way I'm not accustomed to: She wondered what her mother would be like now, whether she is like or unlike how her mom would have been, had she not died. *I know I've said it before, Mom, but I don't*, and my voice cracks, *I can't imagine how you do it, how you've—done it for so many years.* I cry and gasp at almost every word: *I don't know how a person con-continues to wake up e-every day knowing that that that that their mom has—died. How do you—function. I'd be undone. Every single day.*

When we'd replant her mom's grave, we'd also pay respects to the woman whose picture is stuck onto the stone under foggy plastic and to the baby, two rows down.

There was a third thing she made absolutely known: that, after her mother passed, she dreamed that she received a phone call, and her mother was on the other line. And she told my mom all about it in a language she failed to understand by morning.

My mother, now, repeats this old promise: *Just like my mom did. You better believe. If I am able. I will call and let you know that I have arrived.*

■

Kairo's second storyline sees Ryosuke trying to connect to the internet. Rather than a normal home or landing page, despite the error message of the Ur@nus provider, he is taken immediately to a site that displays a series of monochromatic webcams gazing into dark rooms occupied by vague, slow, and lo-fi people.

One stands facing the camera, impossibly slowly shifting his weight from one foot to the other. One sits at his desk, head held in his folded arms, until he slowly lifts and looks directly at the camera, at us, at Ryosuke (hybrid). Ryosuke scoffs or gasps. This sound might register as disgust, except the man we (*we*) see is not disgusting, the room is not disgusting. Instead, what Ryosuke recognizes in this moment is that he is being seen too: the gaze, this alarming, dramatic, this uncanny gaze. The next cam shows a person walking from one side of the small room to the other, silhouetted by a lamp on the desk behind.

Critics describe these webcam individuals as *lonely people* who exhibit *bizarre behaviors*. I admit, though, that I cannot see what exactly is *bizarre* about standing alone in a room, about standing when we are alone, about being so despondent that we sit with our head in our arms or roll across the tatami. The behaviors, anyway, are certainly not unusual—any one of us might do the same. And it is this observation that makes it clear that they are, with only one exception, completely unaware of us, unaware of the gaze pressing in upon them to witness their private dejections. We are discomfited, Ryosuke is, because they are not performers and are not performing.

Here, Ryosuke is the hijacker and terrorist, a transgressor and intruder, not them.

Then:

WOULD YOU LIKE TO MEET A GHOST?

Ryosuke has none of it, shutting off the monitor and slapping away his mouse and keyboard. He lights a cigarette and *Stupid crap*.

To have answered the question at all would have admitted his addressability. His reaction, the fright of being interpolated into a *circuitry* where we exist as always reciprocal: We are each both subject and object on two opposing screens simultaneously—subject and virtual subject. Tapped tapping.

What Ryosuke reacts to is the ambivalence and threat of that question: Either those individuals he's already seen are the *ghosts* he could meet, or, worse, the preceding images, disturbing in their own right, were not of *ghosts* at all. If, then.

Whether the ghosts are abject or Ryosuke is, to give any response in this situation would mean desubjectification, obliteration of self.

K: *If I acknowledge it, it annihilates me.*

I am, only in relation to an object. When *you* is abject, *I* is not at all. (Abject, never an object or a subject, so never a second person.)

■

The first time I wanted to leave my ex or thought I *should* leave him was when he said, *I'm not a feminist* (my pending queerness rejecting his reactionary conservatism). Smoking with him on the back stairwell, my entire insides rejected him, churned against him. *It isn't that I don't think women should have equal rights, it's that I think everyone should have equal rights. I don't like labels. Labels like that don't mean anything anyway. I don't like it when people have to figure out who they are by adopting labels, that's so immature.*

Later, under very different circumstances, when my body again vibrated with antipathy, I called my mother. *I need to leave.*

What do you mean.

I mean I need to leave here right now. I need to go.

Well, call your brother—he's the only one who can help with that.

So I did. *I want to come home. Can you help me*, and he couldn't.

If you really want to come back home, you'll make it happen.

But I'm asking for help. I couldn't yet explain that, if I had tried to make it happen on my own, if I was *seen* trying to make it happen, I would be hurt. I would be killed. I had no way of showing him, *I'm in imminent danger.* That leaving would be an action taken against him to which he'd react. That leaving is the most dangerous time. I needed some kind of extraction *ex machina.*

■

I search for names and BEHEAD. I'm searching for a video, but, to reduce the time dedicated to grimacing at pixelations, gray, and blurs under which lay bodies and blood and swords, I click on IMAGES. This is more efficient and effective: Thumbnails of videos last longer on the internet than do the videos themselves, the removal of the latter neither supposing nor requiring the removal of the former.

I use Wikipedia's list of released beheading videos to exhaust possible names.

SHAMIL ODAMANOV BEHEAD

The red of his shirt seems like blood, and the white fabric covering his mouth seems a continuation of his pallor, looks like all one continuous abject mandiblelessness. I close the search, and I know that his is not the video I once saw.

NIKOLAY MELNIK BEHEAD

Even after clicking SEE MORE ANYWAY, I don't know what this person looks like. I used Cyrillic to search again. I let Google translate two articles from Russian, and I don't know still. No matter how or what I search, I cannot find a face of a man about to be decapitated or who is already.

PIOTR STANCZAK BEHEAD

Not unlike. But he is outside, seated, and flanked by two masked men with guns. In each image, his head is tilted, slightly, to one side or the other. In all, his head is attached to his body. His eyes are black with shadow. It is the eyes, though, that will let me know I have found *it*, the one.

■

In a suicide prevention seminar, we watched an interview with a man who jumped off the Golden Gate Bridge. He explains the experience with clarity and detail: The regret was immediate, he fell for four seconds before hitting the water, his body was traveling at seventy-five miles per hour. His trauma was physics.

My violence recovery therapist once asked me why I always try to intellectualize my experiences, the violence from which I am recovering. I relate to math or biology in an attempt to conjure black and white. Binary is clear in a world where nothing is: There must be a capital-G Good, a right and wrong, threats and non-threats. Where there isn't, I'll make it.

But maybe, despite the masochism of psychoanalysis or therapy in general, intellectualizing is necessary. Maybe doing so protects our psyches from the experiences—the trauma, the abuse, the pain, the horror—by making them anterior to our selves. The answers, the explanations are not within me and, more importantly, never were, and were never meant to be housed by or in my body.

His abuse was never mine to own or explain. (*It isn't yours to explain.*)

It's that, over there, right here in front of me.

This is why I am drawn to theory—my wounds. To psychoanalysis, for granting me metaphors I already know how to use. To K, especially, for the challenge, the impenetrability, the work. To K, because I've been made to believe that I have to do it on my own anyway.

■

In the video, *the* video, the eyes were visible. They were blue, and they were open—either because eyelids naturally drift open after death or because he never closed them, choosing instead to look, to watch. (What does he see.) The whites of the eyes somehow disappeared while those blue irises remained. So I keep searching, because I can't tell what color Piotr Stanczak's eyes were.

A TUNISIAN MAN WAS BEHEADED FOR CONVERTING TO CHRISTIANITY not only needs a citation but also doesn't give me enough critical keywords to search meaningfully.

The video I am looking for is not of James Foley, Steven Sotloff, David Cawthorne Haines, or Alan Henning. These are part of Larson's *seven*, the ones *we all know*—the ones that are conjured with *every* BEHEAD, no matter the other search terms, no matter the quotation marks and date ranges.

But Hervé Gourdel's head is held by the hair. Hervé's eyes are so dark that his face seems white in contrast, except for the mouth down, which is just red. His is the first I see without a body, today, since I saw the video. This is also the first video I've seen today that I can directly download.

THE VIDEO ITSELF MAY BE DOWNLOADED HERE. IT IS GRAPHIC.

■

Years after, in violence recovery therapy, my therapist made it clear just how thoroughly, how early in the relationship my ex had conditioned me for the abuses to come. Survivors are frequently subjected to these horrible videos and images—that is a common tactic. It is both a way to test the survivor's tolerance of violence and a way to desensitize the person to more extreme forms of abuse—skewing our perception so that, no matter what is done to us, we will be grateful that it wasn't anything worse. Or, more likely, believe that what's happening isn't bad in the first place.

He was always proud of how different he thought he was, how dark his aesthetic is, that I wouldn't get it, that not many people get it—that kind of teen rebellion and drive toward individuation he never grew out of. This was especially true of the music he liked, that he played for me.

The video for Angelspit's "Toxic Girl" is un-hostable on YouTube and opens with a standard disclaimer and mature audiences warning, overlaid with a VHS tracking visual effect. It cuts between two distinct sets of narrative: first, a call-now advertisement on KWSK TV, hosted by a Max Headroom type (circa the signal-jacking incident in Chicago, not the television show), for the Toxic Girl, a sex doll; and, second, video of three individuals who have purchased it.

The doll is maybe two feet, just a head and torso, limbless, covered in what is meant to look like a latex suit, exposing only lashed eyes, breasts, and open mouth. The advertisement tells us the product is *easy to handle* and *body odour free*. She comes with a *free workout DVD*. Her primary feature is being *a whore who always wants more*. She *swallows sperm*, so we can *cum anytime, anywhere*. As if we are self-conscious (we are), we are assured that there is *no need for shaved genitals*. Or perhaps it is her mouth that is meant to supplant her own shaved genitals, omitted from the doll.

Either for the supposed sake of television modesty or to intentionally juxtapose the vulgar images, we are also given these quippy euphemisms in the scrolling banner at the bottom of the screen:

SHE'LL SUCK THE CREAM RIGHT OUTTA YOUR CANNOLI
GOBBLE DOWN YOUR GABAGOOL
STUFF HER PUNANI WITH YOUR PANINI
PLAY NOOKY WITH HER SNOOKY

These phrases are cavalier in how they belie the violence of the lyrics and the visuals: The Toxic Girl is either only purchased by those with suicidal ideation or Toxic Girl is the cause of it.

One customer is seen in his bedroom, walls adorned with Japanese video game posters and anime; we see on his laptop screen that he is watching hentai. Another is in a suit, doing coke and drinking Jim Beam. The third is a woman in a bathtub, the mirror over the sink is broken, and a cockroach is in the basin. The first drops his pants then his underwear, Toxic Girl on his desk, soon to be used as expected. The second partially undresses and turns a framed image of himself with his infant son facedown before doing the same. The third brings Toxic Girl into the bath. Then the first takes a bottle of pills. Then the second sticks a handgun in Toxic Girl's open mouth before putting it in his own and firing. Then the third reaches down for a piece of broken mirror and cuts her wrist.

I simply couldn't have understood the merit, the value of the song or video, its beauty—not according to him. And maybe I didn't. But it certainly didn't signify to me then the way it does now: Look at how the lines between sex and violence are obscured, look at how easy it is to distort consent and agency, look at how sexy suicide is. How much pain we can self-inflict. (And how much more we can endure.)

■

On 9/11, I sat in eighth grade history, first row, two seats back, when the teacher got a call and turned on the news. The rest of the day was a continuous loop of the second collision. I knew that this moment would be important—this war on terror had just, only in that moment, begun. But New York meant nothing to me, skyscrapers meant nothing, these people were nothing to me. Even death didn't really mean anything to me then, only experiencing it through the specter of my grandmother. Besides, we are just vehicles.

What *did* mean to me, what stuck out to me that day and for many years, was how all these documents began to float down from the sky, float like ashes, like poplar seeds, so slowly.

In one of the videos, a person says *holy shit* while recording. Some television news stations bleeped it. A solitary bleep to cover the deaths and the terror. That trauma. A Band-Aid on a car crash.

I had heard, probably from the same individuals responsible for pickle girl, that people jumped. I never saw it though. *Sure*, I thought, but *if it happened, we would have seen it.* Later, I learned that more than two hundred people had jumped.

From a hotel just across from the Towers, two tourists recorded a scene in which the results of impact could be witnessed. These videos were watched as evidence in the trial of Zacarias Moussaoui, one of the individuals responsible for the attacks.

■

Ryosuke visits a campus computer lab. He sits casually next to a student and asks, *Say, can the internet dial you up itself.* The student's reaction suggests not an irritation at the question but at Ryosuke's sudden appearance: *You in computer science.*

No, economics. No relation.

Sounds like a hacker. This catches the attention of the graduate student instructor.

It said, "Do you want to meet a ghost." Some website like that. The student is unimpressed and continues to focus on his work, so Ryosuke gets up to walk around the room, flipping pages of open textbooks.

The instructor approaches him and asks, *Which website was that. Something about meeting ghosts*, more interested than the student. *Know the address.*

What. Um . . . address.

I see. Open the Explorer log . . .

Oh, no, no, I really don't know anything about computers.

She gives him instructions, should the site appear again. *Not so fast.* Ryosuke grabs paper and slowly writes down what she says.

Click on it. To bookmark it. If that doesn't work, you know the Print Screen key. Try pressing it. The bell rings and students flood into the room. *Let me know.*

■

Months have passed. That I haven't found the video does not mean it no longer exists. (It must.) But I've stopped searching altogether: The file may be so old that even the PNG doesn't filter into SEE MORE RESULTS.

But I may also have been looking in all the wrong places: What I thought was a terror-era video may have been a cartel video. The sword I recall may have been a knife; the sawing, any other action.

Honestly, I can't even recall most of the video—just the slack of the jaw, how gravity let it fall open to reveal the tongue that wagged with the movement of the murderer's hair-filled fist. I can't actually recall the eyes, only that I *said* they were blue, that I've always said they were blue.

It's possible, too, that I *did* find it (Hervé, James, Piotr) without having recognized or admitted it. Maybe when we're faced with the abject, we reset or reboot; maybe we go face-blind and dissociate.

Nonetheless, the search seemed necessary at first, and for more than pissing off my professor: find-to-reject, reject-to-affirm, *other* so that *self.* The video was the moment I realized the infinitude of the internet, where everything is accessible, especially if it shouldn't be. It was the moment I saw that *right and wrong* is exponentially more difficult than how my mother taught it, than how my idealistic self wished it to be.

To have found it (and maybe the search itself) would have been an opportunity to repeat and work through: I could revisit that dorm room, conveniently divided so that the two who would watch were separated from the three who did not; I could practice the search enough to get myself right up to that edge; I could practice listening to my silent and still body in that moment to react appropriately; I could repeat the watching until I am able to stop it rather than see it through; I could perfect it all until I don't press play, until my friend and I don't have to shuffle into the other room to report our immediate regret and despair.

And maybe finding and watching it could have resensitized me to the violences against me.

■

Kerekes and Slater suggest we need these daily iterations of death and atrocity: *We look to them fitfully in search of a pattern.* We are occasionally so struck, so ab-jected by an atrocity that we, *we*, unite under one superego and become a collective voice of outrage: *The likes of Nick Berg, Dnepropetrovsk Maniacs and Luka Magnotta come along to wake us all up again and reignite some semblance of humanity.*

■

Derek Chauvin's trial aired last week. The event itself was sensational news, literally spectacular, but this wasn't all. We were also given yet another countdown, another exclusive movie premier: a previously unreleased video of Chauvin murdering George Floyd. While the courtroom was given an unedited version (evidence), the simultaneously released public version featured a blurred face. Floyd's body, suddenly fragmented, and we, pushed further *beyond the limit*.

The blur, the gray blob of censorship—I don't know what it's *really* for. I know that, especially in cases of death, we tell ourselves it is added out of respect for the victims and their families. My partner asks me, *If we don't have that expectation of privacy, then why.* The respect is part of that illusion of having a right to privacy in public.

Wayne Koestenbaum says humiliation is a system, a triangle: tyrant, victim, witness. Maybe we censor, indeed, because we think it is possible to extract the victim from this system. We think censorship hides the death (the humiliation) of the actual human victim, as a state of indisposition. If death is final, if there is a limit and boundary that keeps the dead dead, then this censorship cannot save the victim and cannot protect the witness.

Blurring a dead face hides the corpse from view, obscures the fact. This denial does not honor the person or their family. Instead, censoring the face is a way to ask us, each of us our own child, to leave the room during a graphic scene. We believe we can hide our vulnerable and impressionable from some particular trauma. To self-preserve in the face, as it were, of someone else's abjection.

Of course, it's not so simple as a tyrant humiliating a victim only if there is a witness. Not when a tyrant forces their victim to be the witness to another's humiliation, in which case the witness is the victim, humiliated because they can stop neither their own nor the other's humiliation.

■

Under the threat of breaking privacy or security laws, images of the 2004 Madrid bombing were re-uploaded, censored. No laws were being broken. But in 2007 Britain responded to the happy-slapping pandemic by legally banning the recording or distribution of recorded acts of violence.

As far as I can tell, it is not against the law to watch—perhaps because, now, we are so often unwitting participants in the humiliation, subjects who are agencyless in the triangulation, pranked and tricked into witnessing, in a society where depictions of atrocity are simultaneously a legal and ideological necessity.

■

When the video was shorter, viral, memeable, when the video depicted only his suffering, depicted him as breathless gasping desperate for air calling for his mother when the video only indexed his death as impending, his *future corpse*, his face was not blurred. We blur the dead face because it threatens our identity.

In this case, maybe a white identity. In her analysis of Nella Larsen's *Passing*, Judith Butler explains that we formulate who we are by putting ourselves near to those who are *un*like to assert that very unlikeness. In the case of this novella, whiteness can only be asserted in relation to Blackness; John Bellew *needed* to be close to his passing wife, Clare Kendry, for that contrast.

This disavowal is akin to abjection: To create the subject, we eject (defenestrate, in the case of *Passing*) that which could contaminate that *clean and proper* self. We need that abject to always threaten us to maintain that subjectivity: When it's not threatening, we aim to keep it nearby. We are nothing without our relationships to taboos.

The *censored* video from George Floyd's murder is *not* viral. My suspicion is that Chauvin's (and a larger population's) whiteness is rendered invisible when we censor or cut out Floyd, so there is no ideological or political need to disseminate it. There isn't a *message* in it anymore.

Every censorship, every blur fails, even the most extreme image cropping fails to protect us from the message we received from the first 1.4 billion times we (*we*) watched it. In our time of news anchors with over-the-shoulder graphics, we certainly understand that meaning does not lie in the face itself; meaning is always already in the context, in the history. And we can't unlearn our semiotics.

■

The next time Ryosuke's computer connects itself to the internet, it pulls up what must be the same website, despite some differences: The Next button in the bottom right corner to skip through the cams has disappeared, playing only this livestream of a man in a red shirt, something covering his head.

Ryosuke drops his mug and magazine on the kitchen table and rushes over to the computer. *What do I do now.* He follows the instructions he was given: *Click it, and bookmark it.* He receives an error message. *Doesn't work. If that doesn't work, press the Print Screen key.* On the monitor, we see this man in red roll his chair slowly toward the camera and off-screen, to the right. While he is disappearing, he is reappearing on the opposite side of the screen, framing for just a moment the back wall, on which is written *tasukete*, over and over. Closer to us now and as slowly as internet video from the late nineties, he lifts an arm, reaches toward the back of his head, and peels off the black plastic that should have been suffocating him. (Hostage to whom.) It stretches and creates a vacuum, clinging to the jaw line, the cheekbones.

The man's neck is revealed, then his chin, then Ryosuke shuts off the monitor, refusing that potential connection. Perhaps because that shrouded face already signified horror; perhaps because he was unable to bear the gaze from underneath.

■

K makes the word *corpse* synonymous with *cadaver*, which she notes simply as coming from *cadere*, meaning *to fall down*—a euphemism. We started using this word in English in the sixteenth century. As early as the second century, it signified flesh (*caro*) *subsumed by death*. The folk have it, though, that the word comes from *caro data vermibus*, or *flesh for worms*.

Corpse, on the other hand, relates to neither death nor worms. Its root, long gone since Latin, referred to the body, the trunk—mortality, irrelevant. Now, the word refers exclusively to the dead body—no relation to the person it once housed.

When my body *falls*, *I* do not. The *body* is consumed by worms and subsumed by death. Death, fundamentally no relation to *me* at all.

■

Chauvin's trial, like everything, was marked by the pandemic. The image of him we were fed before the trial, the cropped image of his face at the crime scene, was replaced by the current image of his masked face in court, and that mask made him no less recognizable. Of course, he was identified on screen, identified by being in the courtroom for his own trial—there was never any doubt. But I couldn't stop looking at his eyebrows, how obvious, how telling they were, how this sliver of his face was so identifiable. Even without his kneeling on George Floyd, even without his entire face, the message isn't gone.

Many claimed that wearing masks was uncomfortable—their pathetic appropriation of *I can't breathe*. Maybe it wasn't uncomfortable, for me, but it was certainly disconcerting: I can't read your lips, how will my students read my lips, to whom am I speaking, is that a smile or a scowl, a half-face is a distorted face, and this violates the neural template I've made, this uncanny *gaze*.

Arbitrary or not, we depend on difference for meaning. *Erasing of differences, threat to identity.* Abject.

■

In the Deep South, mask-wearing was not only a means of keeping us all healthy and safe but also a way to identify our imagined enemies: At the grocery store, I'd be one of only a few wearing one—not yet even loosely required in Louisiana. From over the produce, I'd feel the intense stare of this unmasked person, feel their rage quiver through the tubers at me. My queer body in this space suddenly queerer, both more threatening and more threatened.

As the pandemic raged on, everything became virtual, and I was maybe not uncomfortable but embarrassed still. Required visual presence on Zoom contracted me back into the body sitting at the dining room table, a stronger sense than what I'd ever felt in person, always believing I was something more than (other than) my vehicle. I was reduced to my portrait. Zoom emphasized this body and this (*gay*) voice, hyperbolized my not-rightly-fit teeth whistling directly into the microphone.

And I watched as my queer, progressive, or compassionate peers and faculty used Zoom to announce their pronouns—to each other and to their students. Being so tightly pulled back into this body prevented me from typing the pronouns I'd come to use—my cis body, despite all the dysmorphia I'm still trying to understand, not yet queer enough.

■

The struggle of writing this imaginary book about our relationship to digitalia is that the opposing object doesn't do anything. The problem is that our relationship is never with the screen at all. The problem: A relationship with the screen is necessarily a relationship with others. Problem: It's a relationship in which only one or neither of us is present—you relate to absent-me, and I relate to absent-you through my own absence. The problem: The relationship is not between bodies or people but only between subjects.

■

Louis Althusser was the first I'd heard use the term *subject* in this way: He says concrete individuals are *hailed* as *concrete subjects*.

Show, don't tell.

His example is a police officer yelling, *Hey, you there*. Whether we turn around or choose to run, we demonstrate our subjectivity—it's our addressability. *Subject*, for Althusser, means *one who is subjectified* or *subjected to something*—subject, he says, because I *accept my subjection*. He uses the French *sujet* as it more directly relates to its Latin root, *subjectus* or *subicio*: forged, counterfeited, prompted, placed under, submitted, literally thrown under.

Fine.

More comfortably for me, now: The *subject* is also the performer of a sentence, the *doer* of verbs, a theme, a cause, a topic. The subject, all our *subjects*, for each of us, is *I*—the speaking subject. *I* is when we represent our budding consciousnesses through something, a word, a letter, that has no relation and bears no resemblance to this waste and that means something for each speaker. That is to say, the subject exists in the symbolic, through and as language.

This does not prove Althusser wrong: We are a subject once we (have the language to) understand that the police officer means *me* when they say *you*.

K: *The subject never is. The subject is only the signifying process and he appears only as a signifying practice.*

■

What K says is this: Our *nature*, our life is *undistinguishable* from the symbolic order; that our body is a *lining*, a shell for that life that exists only because of the Fall, only in sin and language.

And so the body that pollutes who we are necessarily also pollutes language.

An empty shell, *a body without a soul*, is horrible, *unthinkable*. But, and this has been my point, this is no longer (and perhaps never was) limited to the corpse: It applies equally to an otherwise (vacant) living body. Maybe something bestial, something ethereal, something virtual.

So what now—what would Julia say, now, on Scruff, on the internet, into the abyss of Zoom. Do we *perform* or *signify* differently in relation to the screen, on the internet. Are we subjects in isolation. What now, now that my subjectivity is lined by binary rather than a body (lined, of course, by its own binary), my subject wrapped in a shell of electronics rather than flesh.

■

The World Wide Web is subject to geoblocking, the ability for sites to block users and traffic from particular countries. Of course, many can and do bypass this without difficulty. But this bottlenecking, this combination of Google-as-entry-point and filters based on location and language, means each country effectively has a different internet.

As folklore, then, the internet has demonstrated not only our (American) xenophobia but also our continued casual homophobia—it replicates, it spreads, it becomes viral, it escapes the screen and enters our lives.

And how easily: A simple *and cocks* added to the video for Three 6 Mafia's "Ridin' Spinners" led eventually to a GIF of a spinning Tetris block accompanied by the same song. Then a stuffed animal in a dryer. Then a GIF of Pee-wee Herman seated in every seat of a circular couch. Anything that could spin was spun to this song for humor. Then in March of 2005, Meatspin was advertised as a place we can *win big* or *learn the real spin on meat*. What we were met with at this site was a GIF from *TS Bitches* of a person's penis spinning a full rotation while they are fucked in the ass, accompanied by a different song, "You Spin Me Round (Like a Record)" by Dead or Alive. The site also featured a counter that would increase with every spin. After forty-five spins, you see in red letters:

YOU ARE OFFICIALLY GAY :-)

In later iterations of the same site and video:

YOUR A FAGGOT

We—the collective, nobody in particular because everyone—set each other's home pages to Meatspin. We left it open to be found upon returning to the computer. In 2013 Benjamin Blouin redirected the entirety of Florida State University's Panama City campus's Wi-Fi, then serving near a thousand students, to the site for half an hour. In 2015 two young boys watched it on the screens at a restaurant in Greenwich, soon telling their mother they saw *something bad*. In 2016 the website appeared on a digital billboard at a bus stop in Sweden. Maria Escalante had to watch the spins for fifteen minutes until her bus arrived. *Officially gay.* But mostly, I think, we just showed each other, *hey, look at this*, and laughed derisively at the queerness and the queerness of the object, the way a body is just meat.

In this way, we are never isolated, solitary users on the internet: We remain addressable whether we input real referential data, fake data, or none at all into our accounts or profiles. We are embodied subjects, still, bound to this vehicle even if we try to escape it. Even if we think we can.

This is a reckoning that distance and virtuality does not preclude our being observed, seen seeing, seen watching. That, despite any possible anonymity, interacting with others in a virtual space also means interacting with people not in the same space; that interacting with a space is also interacting with a people.

The copyright on Meatspin has lapsed, but its memory still exists in the light gray jigsaw piece and THIS PLUGIN IS NOT SUPPORTED of Adobe Flash—there, flanked by porn advertisements and, below, the HTML and BB codes for the *Fake Video Trick* to *prank your friends!*

■

If subjectivity requires a body and subjectivity enables interpersonal communication, then what of all those fake accounts, all the AI-generated content that wasn't sifted through a CONFIRM YOU'RE NOT A ROBOT. What happens to my subjectivity when I message that bot account on AshleyMadison. And what happens when I get a response.

A visitor to a Chaturbate room is subject, too, contracted into a relationship with the host who interacts with them. That is, of course, until that host discovers they can play pre-recorded videos of themselves in the livestream—making an object of themselves that becomes equally subject as it interacts with not necessarily any one visitor to the room. *Hey, you there.*

■

The snuff film does not exist—no one is paying for VHS tapes documenting death. Atrocity websites do, however, generate profit: Funding for these sites is almost exclusively through pornography advertisements because so few companies in other industries would want to be associated with that market, with that content, would want those trolls and sleuths and perverts to set up profiles and wreak probable havoc.

The traffic, the trafficking from atrocity to pornography is (perhaps surprisingly) high. Maybe death makes us horny; maybe it makes us want to be.

■

K: *The eroticization of abjection, and perhaps any abjection to the extent that it is already eroticized, is an attempt at stopping the hemorrhage: a threshold before death, a halt or a respite.*

It's difficult for me to follow her suggestion regarding the *erotic cult of abjection*, this *perversion*, but I know it is to do with castration:

A fetish (according to Freud) is the thing we (boys) focus on to avoid focusing on our potential castrations. It's the thing that returns us as close as possible to this idea that our mom, like us, has a penis. It's the last sacred thing before we found out that she has been castrated. That is, we fetishize underwear or pubic hair because it is the last thing we saw before we saw the vulva for that first time. Gay men (Freud) have taken the (imagined) (phantom) penis itself as the fetishized object. Women, of course, can't have fetishes. (Freud.)

I understand K as suggesting that, rather than or in addition to the underwear, the pubic hair, the whatever is *normally* fetishized, and, rather than the penis itself, the eroticization of the abject stems from the imagined castration itself. That's what we fetishize and desire, that *hemorrhage*, that wound—that we survived it.

■

Shock sites actively collapse the border between what is sexual and what is abject. As with "2 Girls 1 Cup" and Meatspin, these are often nothing more than recontextualized pornography.

Kirk Johnson was a prolific amateur porn artist with many interests or fetishes, including fisting, stretching his anus. In 1999 the website goatse.cx launched from Kansas City as a shock site featuring one image of a man, Johnson, bent over, eight fingers spreading open his anus for the camera—one of over forty similar images he uploaded in 1997 that spread through Usenet and gay porn communities. The shock site traveled the same way as the others (unwitting redirection, dares, and pranks), but Goatse especially enjoyed a legacy of memes including a revamp of the film poster for *The Men Who Stare at Goats*, various faces effectively censoring the image, an ASCII rendition, a *reverse Goatse* image from inside Johnson, some sporting captions like

IT'S NOT OKAY TO BE GAY.

■

Through a series of metaphors and graphs of varying complexity, psychoanalysts, Lacan in particular, have mapped desire as a void, a hole, a recess. Within its depths lies *objet a*, the law of the father, the word of the father, the mythical phallus—language. Ungraspable, inaccessible, despite our attempts. It's the residue of what we gave up to become a subject just as it is the other's desire. Each of us trying to fill the dick-sized hole we now possess.

In these attempts to reach the unreachable, to get at our ultimate desire, we eroticize the rim, the point just before the ungraspable void. It is that event horizon that is the last and closest thing to the actual desire: the mouth and teeth, the eyelids, the corona—the anus.

We desire the breast, the gaze, the letter, the mouth. We desire a person. What we desire is that person *and* that unreachable thing. But when we desire a person, that person is that event horizon. A *no* thing.

Goatse is literally that same rim, an image of a desiring, desirous, desired void. Just as it is desired, it is abjected: What is erotic to one person is adopted wholly as another's disgust.

■

Ryosuke revisits the lab: empty. He goes to the Computer Science Department, into a large open room lined by computer desks and otherwise filled with large cables, so many devices with knobs and buttons and cords and wires reaching up to the ceiling. The instructor comes in, and Ryosuke says *domo*. The hard subs translate this as *hi*. I have no idea what it means, so I google it, finding user bh_so asking the same question on Japanese Language Stack Exchange. This word, it turns out, dates back to a phrase used in the Edo period, *domo nani mo ienu*, which means *unable to speak in spite of oneself* or *I'm unsure of what to say to you* or *I am unsure of who you are.*

Or at least that's the highest-voted answer that serves as an explanation here: *You're the one, um.* Ryosuke confirms and introduces himself awkwardly. She introduces herself as Harue.

How'd it go.

Well, it came back again. And I pressed that Print Screen key.

Can I come over and check it out.

She moves to finish her work before they leave. He interrupts her to ask *What's this*, looking at a computer screen showing white-ish blurry dots floating in blackness, like a microscopic recording of the Tyndall effect, like dust particles we see in light coming through the window.

Something we programmed here. If two dots get too close, they die, but if they get too far apart, they're drawn closer. A miniature model of our world. I wouldn't suggest staring at it too long.

■

The forum cutedeadguys.net may have been late to the game, having been first registered in 2009. Except I'm not even sure if it *is* a shock site. Maybe it's more like an atrocity site, a special interest group. Its forum categories do little to help me figure it out:

INFORMATION & ASSISTANCE
DEATH & MAYHEM
COMMUNITY
NECRO ENTERTAINMENT
SEWAGE

It features the usual cartel and Jihadi beheading videos as well as autopsy footage and crime scene images. Despite so much chatter and excitement about cannibalism in the forum, there is a notable absence of any verifiable depiction of such—this is true, too, of necrophilia. But these are likely such hot commodities that they need to be locked in THE SECRET ROOM for *top notch material submitted by our best posters*.

I look at the *current visitors* and see almost two hundred profiles active in this moment. Most of them are named Guest, unregistered. Half of these individuals are browsing the threads

DEAD WOMEN AND GIRLS COLLECTION
DEAD GIRLS [PART 1]
CHINESE FEMALES
MELANIA TRUMP FLORAL JACKET FROM DOLCE & GABBANA COSTS $51K

The most trafficked media, even on websites focusing on guys, is of women. Perhaps, then, the name *cutedeadguys* is misleading.

The entire premise is ambiguous anyway: *Cute* is meant to elicit a nurturing response, and yet, here, while it seems less lecherous than other adjectives, *cute* is still desirous in nature, perhaps even more so since virtually none of the depicted individuals are *cute* children. I can't tell if there is an implied comma in the title: Are these guys who are both dead and cute, or are they cute, as opposed to ugly, dead guys. It isn't entirely abject, and it isn't entirely erotic either.

As we literally objectify a corpse, make an object of the subject ($O \neq A$), that thin border, between *I* and *undone*, *me* and *not-me*, collapses.

This is either not abject enough, as if it exists in degrees, or an abjection of the abject—so far and deeply into abjection that we circle back around to safety and order. Objectifying a corpse, an attempt to undo the transgression, the disorder.

I was struck by one comment in particular in response to a photograph taken during an autopsy, a regular, legal, necessary autopsy, depicting a surgically opened skull with the organ removed:

I LOVE AN EMPTY BRAIN PAN.

This is why I love language, the way it can mean anything and so means nothing until the very moment we decide how we want it to mean:

I love *an empty brain pan*: sarcasm. Preference for organs. Preference for life.

Love: both *want to be* and *want to have*.

Empty brain pan: the rim, desire, event horizon.

Empty *brain pan*: both strict observation and figuratively assessing intelligence.

I love an empty brain pan: derisive of the desire.

Conflating queer and taboo desires.

Asserting queer desire as taboo.

Asserting dominance over another man.

Dominance over the dead.

Over mortality.

Morality to boot.

Regardless, this all complicates Larson's diatribe: Do the users of such a website make the *death* happen again or the *autopsy*. Do they *make it happen again* or are they conjuring at their desk an already dead corpse—a corpse, rather than a person (subject). Can death be *fancied* over a corpse. Is the individual humiliated or the corpse defiled. (Or desecrated.) Does an autopsy *signify* death, as K says of a wound, *with blood and pus, or the sickly, acrid smell of sweat, of decay*; or is this like the flatline, in the presence of which we can *understand, react, or accept*.

■

In the campus library, Ryosuke passes through the stacks, back and forth, visibly uncertain. He sees Harue reading a book in the next stack. They see each other, and he says, *I don't really use the library much*. When she places the book back in its spot, we see the spine: 幽霊現象.

The hard subs translate the title as *Phantoms*, but there are two words here: *yūrei* and *genshō*. *Ghost Phenomenon*, if we westernize their concept of *faint* or *dim spirit*.

Ryosuke grabs it off the shelf, flips through it, *You reading this. Is it related to your work in the lab.*

Yeah.

Later, in the library, Ryosuke is seated with the open *Ghost Phenomenon*. He reads, *How many ghosts have existed since prehistoric times.*

He's clearly frustrated by the rhetorical question, the academese, and puts the book down. His eyes wander back to the stacks where we see a young boy, pale-faced, color drained, his body bifurcated on screen by the shelf and books immediately before him.

The graduate student Yoshizaki comes to sit next to Ryosuke. They met through Harue in the computer lab: He is the one who developed the *miniature model of our world*, the *only* one who *understands it.*

Do you see it too. Sure you do, because he's really there.

Who is that.

You'll have to catch him to find out. Start right now, and you might succeed. Have a go.

Ryosuke bolts toward the stacks as the young boy slides away to the right, out of frame. Ryosuke follows down the stacks, gets to the other side, passes back and forth, visibly uncertain.

Ryosuke: *He disappeared.*

I see.

The young boy is a ghost, a *yūrei*, and he's really here. The border between life and death, collapsed. The corpse collapses that border too (*death infecting life*), but this isn't that. This is the collapsed border between the living and the afterlife. *Here* and *somewhere else. Not-here.*

As Yoshizaki makes to leave, Ryosuke asks him to wait. *Just what was that.*

In another room, over tea, he explains to Ryosuke that *the spirit or consciousness, the soul, whatever you want to call it—it turns out the realm they inhabit has a finite capacity. Whether that capacity accommodates billions or trillions, eventually, it will run out of space. Once it's filled to the brim, it's got to overflow somehow, somewhere. But where. The souls have no choice but to ooze into another realm, that is to say, our world.*

According to this, the sole explanation, these ghosts are the overflow waste of that other realm. No agency, no will, not even able to be upset; unable to fit there and unfitting here.

How queer.

To stop this, he explains, we use any material we have at hand.

■

It is summer, so there are few classes in session, but the pandemic continues regardless. The halls are dark, mostly, mostly lit only by the sunlight that comes through the occasional floor-to-ceiling window. All the doors are closed. The sound of any movement is always sudden and strange. Just like in the parking garage, where there is always a new car or two, or the same few cars but moved—here, there are only indices of really anyone else being here. Trash accumulates in the bins, and the bins move across the hallway. Blinds open are closed. The slam of a door, the sound of footsteps. But perhaps the cockroaches are more active, dying openly now, in the darkness in the middle of the hall, scurrying not when they hear me come but only when I turn the corner, panicking only long after I have already turned on the restroom light.

The desks that have been pulled from these pandemic classrooms are in tight rows at the top of the stairs. The couches and chairs and tables that have always sat in the hallways have all been marked with signs that say PLEASE CHOOSE A DIFFERENT SEAT and ONLY ONE PERSON PER TABLE. The desks, though, which aren't meant to be in a hallway at all, are marked off with, are cordoned by one long strip of red duct tape stretching over four or five at a time. It's a symbolic gesture: how tightly they are packed into this corner or that, each seat blocking the arm of the next, makes the tape moot, no longer deterring us from sitting but only telling us we can't sit in the chair we can't sit in. Even if the desks were arranged differently, red tape could never stop us from sitting, temporary as it is.

The locks to the restrooms are covered by the same red tape. On these pieces is written PLEASE STOP LOCKING in black permanent marker. Here, another index: first of the sender, then of the implied recipient. And then of me.

■

As Yoshizaki explains this to the shaken Ryosuke, the film cuts to what we can infer to be the first instance of this *overflow*, the first time someone tried to stop the overflow: A man at the Suzuki shipyard asks a construction worker for tape, *anything'll do, some tape*. The construction worker happens to have red duct tape. He offers it and asks, *how's this*. The man seals a window with the tape, then he seals the door from the outside with the same red tape. There—additional space, a waiting room for the ghosts, these emanations to inhabit. There—a taboo for the rest of us. The Forbidden Room.

■

That night, after he strangled me, I had to create my own evidence of trauma: I took photos because I knew I had to. I didn't know yet if I'd file anything, but I knew that, if I ever chose to, I'd need proof. Hard, physical proof—the relationship itself had taught me that my words meant nothing.

My therapist encouraged me to speak to the free Domestic Violence Legal Clinic. I showed up to an enormous carpeted room with reception in the center, sheepishly said I wanted to file a restraining order, and sat alongside these dozens of individuals, these children and mothers mostly, to fill out the paperwork to be granted the order of protection.

With the legal adviser, I restated everything I had just written. Then, while filling out his own forms, he asked, *Do you want to get divorced as well.*

■

In the Computer Science Department again, Harue brings Ryosuke back to the running simulation. It's changed: Two dots flicker as they approach each other and then merge. They move together, it moves as one for a second or two. When she plays it back frame by frame, Ryosuke can see that, for one frame, they split apart, weaker than before, and then merge again. This merging seems uncomfortable: They leave a blur of movement behind and flicker in and out of existence, glitch themselves together and apart again before both fade away entirely.

They're like ghosts.

■

I showed him the pictures of the handprint across my neck, the bruise over my ribs, the gouge of his fingernail on my chest. The broken coffeepot. The broken door.

I kept the images on my computer desktop, at the ready, for a long time. Like the order itself, of which I always kept a folded copy on my person, this evidence was meant to protect me. But, also to protect myself, I made the icons hidden—literally hidden from sight, searchable only if searched for. They weren't uncovered, de-hidden, exhumed until I moved out of state years later, assuming that I would then forever be safe from him.

But they too still exist somewhere deep in a cloud service I no longer use. I just thought to look for them. I'd be searching blindly at this point, because it's no longer as simple as toggling the *show hidden icons* switch. I can do this, for you, to *show* you. And I do not.

■

As a child, Harue began to fear that the system she imagined in which we die and reunite with everyone in the afterlife may not be true. With Ryosuke, in her apartment, she decides that *you might be all alone after death too. That nothing changes with death, just right now, forever. Is that what becoming a ghost is about.*

Ryosuke asks, *What have ghosts got to do with us. Besides, we're alive.*

Harue turns on her many monitors, each showing a different individual from the WOULD YOU LIKE TO MEET A GHOST website. *Then who are they. Are they really alive. How are they different from ghosts.*

In fact, she says, *ghosts and people are the same, whether they are alive or dead.*

(She's right; I know she's right.)

On the internet, we are heterogeneous, just like ghosts: *here, not-here.* As subjects, we are heterogeneous too: semiotic, symbolic. These borders can collapse, and the metaphysical and prelapsarian irrupt into signification. If this were not true, if the semiotic, our cries and vibrations, didn't interrupt or fracture our (symbolic) language, we'd be more like automatons or, indeed, ghosts. Without that energy of subjectivity, we'd essentially be husks. Empty vehicles. Dead.

The director, in that same interview to which all the critics refer, also probably not coincidentally seemingly the only one available in English: Ghosts are *human-like, but all the emotional elements of a normal person are missing. They're empty shells. That's what scares me.*

■

In the remake, *Pulse*, Mattie receives a package from her already deceased boyfriend: red duct tape with a note attached that says, *Red tape keeps them out. Don't know why.* The only explanation as to the *why* of the red duct tape is given by Dexter, when he explains the whole ghost phenomenon, and his role in it, to Mattie: *It was a telecom project. It was super-wide band. We found frequencies that we didn't even know existed, and they came through. . . . We thought it was like a radio wave interference, then we realized that there was a pattern to it. Every time that we'd try to monitor them, they would stop, or they would change frequencies. . . . Red utility tape. It must have blocked part of the spectrum that they needed for transmission, so we could keep them out of a room.*

The ghosts are, in some capacity, data and information, but now we know they are also light. They are intangible enough to come through phone jacks, Ethernet cables, cell phones, but solid enough to be blocked by something as thin as tape. They are between all these states—indeterminate, ambiguous. They cross borders, infect and collapse them. Abject.

The red tape has two purposes, protective and preventive: It warns us of danger and prevents the ghosts' escape. As it is seen among the film's urbanity and monochromatic aesthetic, Jerry White suggests the tape is also a vibrant temptation to transgress.

The tape, and the room itself, the barrier, is the taboo—transgressed both when it is opened from the outside *and* when the abject escapes regardless. The ghosts are abject, but so too is their physics: the cracks through which they escape, because physical but untouchable; the internet, because it delivers but is not any kind of matter we know; everything that could keep the ghosts in is proven porous and fragile. Everything we use to shore up our sense of self, porous and fragile. The self, itself porous and fragile.

■

We collectively imagine a type of person. I've settled, often, for *trolls* and more often characterize them as *mouth-breathers* or *neckbeards*, all horrible epithets, I know. I mean those we imagine and depict as being holed up in their bedrooms, *getting off* on dark-web material, on 4chan, these sleuths and internet perverts—stigmatized for the past forty years in response to the heinous crimes of the Otaku Killer, Tsutomu Miyazaki, the Rat Man, the Little Girl Killer.

■

I watched my peers hold hands with their boyfriends and girlfriends, later kiss and get into each other's cars; I heard the stories of the fucking, the blowjobs, the drinking and meeting people from the next school district over. A privilege I was not afforded.

The age difference between me and my siblings is such that we collectively knew every student to attend our school district from thirteen years my senior to three years younger. This isn't an impressive feat, there being only 150 in a graduating class. We knew everyone, and we knew that, within those years, the only other *openly* queer student was Francis, a whole decade before.

Perhaps Francis and people like him had to beseech a god or some other metaphysical entity until their queer migration to Columbus, Ohio's capital and, to us rural folk, gay mecca. Unlike Francis, I could, for better or worse, worship at the altar of virtuality.

■

Beginning to feel the despondence of Tokyo, the rampant isolation, Harue explains to Ryosuke that she is *scared to be* alone. *Take me somewhere.*

Where to.

Somewhere far away.

They jump the turnstiles and sit on the bench to wait for the train. In the distance, we can see a figure dressed all in black standing on the upper stairs leading back into the station—the same they must have come down just moments before to get to the platform. There is no movement, uncanny or otherwise, no blurring. There is no sound, no handshake, no shrill.

On the train, Harue asks, *Where did everyone go.*

I'm here. I'm here beside you. Even if there's no one else, it doesn't matter. We are both definitely here.

She rests her head on Ryosuke's shoulder just as the empty train comes to a stop.

As Ryosuke stands to find out where or why the train has stopped, Harue decides, *I've got to go back.* She is, perhaps, momentarily panicked. *This is the end of the line.*

That's not true, he says as he stops Harue from running. *It'll start moving. I'll go check with the driver. Promise you'll wait right here.*

But she is resolute: As Ryosuke leaves for the conductor, she runs out of the train.

■

Otaku, according to one of the earliest pieces written about the lifestyle, by Volker Grassmuck, are individuals who *tend toward an isolated and non-human existence.* The word, the identity, began as *those obsessed with anime.* The interest is material (as a physical collection), social, and sexual. Grassmuck infers that the 2-D sexual satisfaction of anime is safer for otaku. It is possible, too, that this kind of sexual satisfaction is a *reaction to the pressure of male chauvinism,* boys refusing to grow into that kind of adult. *They don't like to be aggressive. True, in the comics there is a lot of violence, S/M, lashing, and bondage, but in the real world they could not do it—they are too shy.* Or, alternatively, these characters and scenarios are surrogate for the boy's fetishistic or *chauvinistic* desire.

■

Miyazaki had four victims, girls, ages four to seven: Mari, Masami, Erika, Ayako. They were photographed nude, strangled, dumped in the woods. He took limbs and clothes as trophies. He recorded himself fucking their corpses. He drank blood. He cremated one and mailed the remains, sure to leave intact teeth and bone on top, to her parents. Then he harassed the parents, all.

The media's distorted focus was also applied to fourteen-year-old Boy A (Seito Sakakibara [Shinichiro Azuma]), who killed ten-year-old Ayaka Yamashita and eleven-year-old June Hase. The explanation for atrocity was not in the boy's mental health and history of abuse and animal mutilation; instead, it was in his manga, his porn, and his copy of *Friday the 13th*.

■

Harue clicks through the lo-def webcams that now face into rooms that are empty, empty, empty, empty. Each well lived in, each with computers—bedrooms, offices, all rooms in which a person might appear at any moment but doesn't because almost everyone is gone now, now that we have all become so despondent that we suicide or disintegrate. Then, there is a figure, sitting, silhouette. Then the image fades away to the same that Ryosuke saw, the man in red, the room with *tasukete* written all over the back wall. She taps to Print Screen, presumably like she had instructed Ryosuke to do. The first page to mete out of the printer is the same that Yabe found in Taguchi's apartment: HOW TO MAKE THE FORBIDDEN ROOM. Then the man has pulled off the plastic over his face, and Harue does not look away. As our hybrid subject, we see the eyes seeing us, meeting us. He leans forward, leans back, puts a handgun under his chin, and fires. We don't look away.

The second page that comes out of Harue's printer is the actual instructions for making a Forbidden Room. The printed text is in multiple directions, many diagonals, only diagonals. As is often the case, the hard subs capture little more than essential meaning:

CONSTRUCTION MATERIALS—RED TAPE.

But now, the gift of hyperreality: Google allows us to use the camera on our phones to instantly translate any text that appears to the camera. It replaces the original text with the language of your choice, changing and moving as the image changes and moves, changing as it translates and then translates better, translates partial before whole.

This is a tool more useful for books, for text printed on solid, flat objects. This is for a steady hand and a static text, a still text. It is less useful for text that appears in multiple directions and always a diagonal, less useful for pointing at a computer-screen depiction of a film camera's image of words printed on a page.

To the best of my understanding, formed by scanning the text with Google and compiling its dozens of translations, the instructions page says:

THINGS TO PREPARE

ONLY RED TAPE

DESPAIR TO THE WORLD

CLOSE ALL GAPS

BLACK VINYL

I think that, to those of us who don't speak Japanese, this collectively and impressionistically means: *Use red tape to cover all gaps, unless.*

■

Miyazaki was discovered to have over five thousand VHS tapes of anime and slasher films. The photos and videos he took of and with his victims were collected among these. The popular interpretation was that his *sick sexual desires*, including his reportedly *early* interest in child pornography and his stint capturing upskirt creepshots, motivated him to make his *own, rare video* to collect; but whether that was the intention or not, all of his possessions were subsumed by this VHS collection that engulfed his home. Regardless, the belief became that otaku possessed tendencies that included the *non-human*, necrophilia and pedophilia, and a blanket *fetishism*.

He was linked to the taboo, and to cement that association, we produced and spread rumors that his disfigurement, the bones of his hands and wrists fused together, was the result of incest. Our belief, apparently, that taboo begets taboo.

■

It doesn't seem to me that we fear the isolation caused by our increased use of internet technologies or connectivity. We are afraid because we feel it encroaching upon our self, our subject, because it (and its relationship to the body, the semiotic) is suddenly proven unstable or dissociative. In spite of the isolation, what we fear is, still, infection, contamination, virality.

There were only two mainstream instances of cybersuicide by 2001, but academics and news outlets hemorrhaged their fear around suicide-related material on the web, including pre-suicide diaries (mislabeled as suicide notes), forums for encouragement, and assisted suicide how-tos. The fear was of suicide contagion, of our *vulnerable* copying what they see, joining pacts and wanting to be part of something bigger than themselves, even in or through death. After fifteen more years of this supposedly, folklorically happening, Steven T. Brown shares his observation in *Tokyo Cyberpunk: Posthumanism in Japanese Visual Culture* that *instances of suicide streamed live over the Internet seem to be the preference of those who wish to commit suicide in a private space where authorities are less likely to intervene and at the same time sensationalize the moment via Webcam in order to maximize the number of potential witnesses. It is as if those who commit suicide via Internet videostreaming are seeking some sort of social connection with other people at the very moment their lives are about to end, even if that connection is merely virtual and the contact brief.*

Despite the panic, the health organizations' reports, despite knowing Instagram's unhealthy effects on teens, there is a glaring absence of this phenomenon precisely because the (inadvertent) hosting companies so egregiously minimize the event and prevent its media spread. It took two decades for a case such as this to broadly circulate the news.

TikTok saw two suicides in India between 2016 and 2019.

Ribeiro reports for *The Intercept* that in 2019, 280 people watched a young man from Brazil kill himself on TikTok. An hour and a half later, TikTok became aware. The objective cell phone camera continued recording, and TikTok continued watching this man's corpse for three more hours, during which they discussed their diversion tactics before calling the police.

In 2020 Ronnie McNutt opened a Facebook livestream. According to his friend in the audience, Joshua Steen, he was drunk, and he had a shotgun. After McNutt fired it (or misfired), the police were called, and Facebook was asked to close the stream. McNutt answered a phone call, argued. *Hey guys, I guess that's it.* Then he took the shotgun and fired again. Then Steen received Facebook's reply:

THIS POST WILL REMAIN ON FACEBOOK BECAUSE WE ONLY REMOVE CONTENT THAT GOES AGAINST OUR COMMUNITY STANDARDS. OUR STANDARDS DON'T ALLOW THINGS THAT ENCOURAGE SUICIDE OR SELF-INJURY.

■

Miyazaki was found guilty of all his crimes, despite his claims to insanity, including the delusion that a Rat Man was the culprit, not himself. This, no different from Magnotta's Manny. The defense counsel argued that *the audiovisual culture of videotapes and television, the lack of a sense of reality in the information society and the isolation of youth are behind the crime as sickness of modern society.* The statement seems ludicrous to me now, when we are all isolated and reality is even more distant due to the pandemic, when our current culture is of the internet and, in effect, our sense of reality is distorted by machines of *dis*information.

Miyazaki was hanged in 2008. It is rumored that his remains are buried in an unnamed ossuary with the rest of the unclaimed death row inmates—isolated, now, forever, alongside these other unmarked, unvisited and unvisitable ghosts.

Two years later, Justice Minister Keiko Chiba opened the Tokyo Detention House's execution chamber to the media for the very first time. While researching this, the aftermath and effect on otaku, these pictures began to appear of the chamber, the same in which Miyazaki himself was hanged. The room is wood-paneled, carpeted, hooks in the wall, pulley in the ceiling. The trapdoor is marked off by red duct tape along all four sides; the inmate stands in the center of this, also marked in red duct tape. These concentric squares of red tape are, to my eye, identical to the first character in the word *kairo*:

回

To return to, to reply.

■

He taught me about Tor browsers, which tout their anonymity, like the much more popularized VPNs or more secure browsers like

DuckDuckGo, but also grant access to the dark web—overlay networks existing on top of our own internet—a difficult-to-learn and navigate series of addresses ending in .onion. Tor browsers are meant for privacy, but, often, downloading and using such software signals to authorities that you are otaku, a terrorist or child abuser.

This demonstrated to me his apparent internet savvy; this demonstrated to him my acceptance of incremental subjection, to something more, more extreme. He told me to use Hidden Wiki to find the dark-web directories—necessary, since there is no googling there, no Google. Instead, you have to know what you want to find and to see. Here, literally everything is *iykyk* or, more accurately, *if you know, you know how to find it*. Now, as I understand it, it's mostly Bitcoin and drug sites, but I recall being disappointed then too: I'd already seen worse, quotidian porn sites host worse, there's worse on the news. Perhaps the only interesting bit of information I saw, then, was a list of costs for hitman services. Although I couldn't have afforded it, $30,000 to castrate someone seemed inexpensive to me.

■

Otaku now commonly refers to those who are so invested in and obsessed with the internet that they *reside both virtually* there *and physically within the confines of their dark cluttered bedrooms*—a term people use for themselves, despite the (still lingering) stigma. It's subversive: Theirs is a *mode of being outside oneself without being out of one's mind, of being dispersed in cyberspace and still finding life worth living*. They are the best of the (already dead) postmodern. No reason to despair the pandemic.

Theirs is a culture where information is the only available material—knowledge the only currency. Magnotta called them *armchair lonely internet users*, but now, even *more* recently (because of the pandemic, perhaps; because of the cell phone, perhaps), these individuals are armchair detectives, internet sleuths, and suburban moms who, according to their portrayal in the media, are trying to spice up their humdrum lives.

■

In 2015 Larson couldn't have seen the video, but I would like to know what she has to say, now, about the virality of abjection.

George Floyd's death ignited not only a summer of protests but also a rhetorical debate on the appropriateness, the effect, of such violent videos:

WHOSE DEATHS WE AFFORD PRIVACY AND WHOSE WE DON'T
VIDEOS OF POLICE KILLINGS ARE NUMBING US TO THE SPECTACLE OF BLACK DEATH
CELLPHONE VIDEOS OF BLACK PEOPLE'S DEATHS SHOULD BE CONSIDERED SACRED, LIKE LYNCHING PHOTOGRAPHS
VIDEOS OF POLICE BRUTALITY TRAUMATIZE AFRICAN AMERICANS
DON'T SHARE VIDEOS OF GEORGE FLOYD'S DEATH, DO THIS INSTEAD

We are told to *stop viewing footage of Black people dying so casually* while we are being casually shown those same videos on the news, while the videos autoplay on social media, while more and different videos of violence against Black people are *leaked*, out of both an attempt to raise awareness *and* out of a lack of empathy.

I want to hear Larson talk about how videos of white men on their knees come in at least two types based on agency (subjects, objects).

■

A corpse (*utmost*, not) represents the *fundamental pollution*. Of what.

The answer is not *life*—we aren't seeing life polluted by death. Maybe we are, but that's not K's claim. An encounter with a body without a soul is a realization that *I*, *me*, is polluted by a body—that the body is a vehicle for my *me*, a vessel that is indistinguishable from the symbolic.

I am (indistinct from) language.

To the best of my knowledge, it remains critically unstated in K's work that the abjectness of a soulless body implies that we think that *that* body ought to have a soul. This abjection implies that we identify with the subject, the soul enough for it to register as a threat to *me*. That is, these atrocities are not harmful to our psyches or subjectivity if they are inflicted upon people who I think are *unlike* me or things I don't even consider to be *people*, animals and the dehumanized alike.

■

The problem of a beheading video, of watching one, is not the beheading. In fact, we regularly commodify death, replay it, click it; we mobilize under it.

The problem of a beheading video is with abjection, a refusal of and a threat to the order we've deemed natural: What we know belongs inside comes out, we say *we don't do that* but we do; while the white man is on his knees, the colonial mind of Larson's audience, *we*, me and maybe you, reject his sudden status as object rather than subject.

And yet, the numbers. The 44.8 million of us, *we*, who stopped watching, who clicked to close, who backspaced our refusal of the moment of death, of the insides-out: This number still needs to be reconciled.

■

Once, during a fight, my ex took a knife and locked himself in our bathroom. Maybe it was *I can't live without you*. Maybe *you can't live without me*. Either way, it was punitive—manipulative in the most obvious way. And I had no choice but to play the part.

I did: I fucking flat-palmed that door (hardwood) and demanded to be let in. I frantically shook and turned the handle. I threatened to call the police. I cried and begged him not to hurt himself, gently, calmly, unangered, unafraid—and so very afraid that my performance was insufficient. I called the police and cried at them, knowing he'd be listening to determine whether I was really calling or only pretending to. But I had also been so tired for so long, tired, abused, and wounded: *At this point, you know I can't stop you. You won. Except I know that if you* really *wanted to do this, you wouldn't need to lock yourself in a bathroom.*

So when the police arrived and buzzed the broken buzzer, I left the apartment, bathroom still locked, ex still inside, silent, and walked to let the officers into the building's foyer. *What's going on.* I explained the situation and added that I suspected he was faking it. *If we go up there, we will admit him. And he will not be able to check himself out. Do you understand.* Yes. *Do you want us to go up.*

I suddenly understood that this was a way out—his own manipulation tactic, my salvation. His fantasy was so real now, that it was no longer his to control. What we couldn't see happening was treated as if it were. Schrödinger's suicide. I didn't cry at the officers anymore.

■

The channel airing the trial has stopped sharing the digitally displayed evidence altogether, censored or otherwise.

Finally, we have shut our eyes. *Finally*, not said out of relief: We shut our eyes because we have seen it all already. Finally, no longer a dead face to see.

■

Our perspective set behind her, we don't see Harue's reaction as she clicks away from the scene, her body stiff and still. The monitor, the computer screen, the screen on which we watch the film, displays a new camera. It's Harue's bedroom, pointing out the door into the next room, in which Harue sits at her computer, her back to this new camera, having just clicked away from the man in red shooting himself. The perspective shifts irregularly, as if another glitch, as if there are multiple cams competing for dominance. She can be seen through the doorway, then she can't be seen—closing one eye and then the other. Camera 1, camera 2. She approaches slowly, cautiously.

I'm not alone.

Harue literally embraces the formless, invisible entity that watches her and by extension her audience who is (who may be) watching this embrace. Now, unafraid of the voyeur, this internet ghost.

We are always already exactly as fragmented as they.

■

I'm not as certain as others that virtual communities and digital interpersonal communications are a form of alienation. It seems to me that there is suddenly a community for everyone, a way to connect with individuals we'd never have met, never encountered. It seems to me that we have access, suddenly, to a greater number of communities, no matter how small, no matter how specific. As with cybersuicide, it just makes clear that we want to be valued by being acknowledged and witnessed.

■

By the time the police went up, he had gone—unlocked the bathroom doors, now wide open, returned the knife to its proper place, and left. *Where is he. Do you know where he could have gone.* No, I don't know. But he must have left through the back door, there.

They didn't look out that door, they didn't search for him. Instead, they left with only, *One more call, and he's being admitted. Doesn't matter why you call. Do you understand.*

So simple.

And I had never thought of it before.

■

Ryosuke's search for Harue continues into the morning, and we see him wander an empty Tokyo neighborhood, exhausted. He stops at a broken corner vending machine, cans spilling out onto the ground. From across the street, he sees Michi, from the other storyline. He approaches and hands her a soda.

Michi: *What are you doing here.* Unable to answer, Ryosuke asks her the same, but she has no answer either. They sit together to drink their sodas.

Ryosuke: *So many things happened at once, it's impossible to sort them all out.*

Yeah.

They try to learn about each other as they work to fix Michi's car:

So you're a student.

Yeah. You.

I had a job.

Amazing.

Did you have any friends.

Maybe one, I guess.

What was she like.

What. I don't really know. I never really found out.

Where is she.

Somewhere.

Inspired, like Junco was, Michi asks, *Why don't you look for her. She's still somewhere, right. Let's go find her.*

■

Once, after getting fucked on cam, it was requested that I be pissed on, so that's what happened. We had finally found someone who could watch us in private for however long this person wished. It was requested, then, that we shower, so we did. When my ex was done, he stepped out, dried off behind the computer placed on the toilet lid. As I said some version of *goodbye we're done now* to the person elsewhere, he told me to *make money*, to stay. *But I'm done too.* He told me to do whatever this person says, *even if it means you just sit there and talk to him.*

He went to smoke, and I did, I stayed and talked to this person. When he came back inside, he stood in the doorway and talked to me, I can't remember about what, but I remember trying to communicate with and acknowledge him without giving the elsewhere person on the computer the impression that my attention was anywhere but on them and the time for which they were paying. My ex was furious that I would put another person before him, literally in front of him. *But you told me to*, and that didn't matter. He pinned my wet, naked body down with his cross-armed stare, there, behind the laptop, watching me watching him watching me being watched by someone else entirely, triangulating my body into yet another humiliation.

He told me to keep going, again, more, and I did, and he just continued to watch me talk to this person about nothing in particular—they were just lonely.

■

Having fixed the car, Ryosuke and Michi start searching for his friend, Harue. Approaching her apartment, Ryosuke announces that this is their *last stop. Then we'll go as far as we can.*

In Harue's apartment, Michi picks through the computer desks as Ryosuke stands in the bedroom staring at *tasukete* written over and over on the wall. Michi comes into the room and looks out the window. *An abandoned factory.* Ryosuke: *I wonder.*

Walking through this wrought and arid building, they see a woman in red standing on a scaffold. Her head is covered in black plastic. It's Harue, and they run up to where she should be but isn't and find a roll of red duct tape.

Harue slowly steps into sight. She stops, stands, raises her left arm behind her head and peels off the plastic in the same manner as the man in red. She holds a pistol in her right.

Ryosuke: *Let's get out of this place, together.*

Harue: *Together.*

Yeah.

Harue grabs something from a nearby basket and tosses it above her.

Something like silver confetti falls between them. Just as Ryosuke asks her to hand over the gun, she picks it up, points it up under her chin, and fires.

Back in the car, Ryosuke says, *We couldn't save her* and rests his head on Michi's shoulder.

■

When real-time location sharing became available for our phones, my ex insisted that we use it, excited to make sure I didn't cheat on him while he was at work. Obviously, real-time location sharing is also location *tracking*, a tool for abuse in relationships.

Perhaps only because I could, I watched his icon scoot across Chicago, noting any deviance, any deviation from his route: glitches, electronic and ethereal miscommunication, lags. Meanwhile, likely because of my cheap phone service (discounted even more for my SNAP benefits), *my* icon was firmly placed in Winnetka, a suburb that lies a difficult two and a half hours, seven and a half miles north.

The *blips*, avatars, and map pins, like Fleischmann's, do *travel* and so may *follow*. Again, the data, light and triangulation, the binary is agent. And yet, none of it has anything to do with our bodies.

You need to explain why the fuck you were there.

I wasn't.

You can't lie. Google said you were.

But it still shows I'm there. I'm here, not there.

Who the fuck was he.

In these moments, he often screamed racial epithets and disparaged my supposedly loose hole. (He was both racist, it turned out, and the epitome of small dick energy.) He manufactured the pain and insult of my enjoying being stretched open, permanently altered, marked, used by another man without him, in spite of him. Making a narrative of my body, finding imagined answers there to his delusional questioning. He delighted in it, using his body to imitate the roughest fucking and my own supposed cries of bliss. The scrutiny of both my actual and virtual bodies. Fucking humiliating.

A different therapist, before, had noted our body language: I shrank in the chair next to him, crumpled myself up, smaller than him, always.

The questions remain there, here, inside. I feel them, even now, churning inside like snakes. Even now, a decade later, 1,300 miles away, when my partner asks, *How was your day.*

■

They need gas. Back in the abandoned factory, where they found Harue and where Harue killed herself, Ryosuke drops the cap of the gas can, and it rolls into a Forbidden Room, already opened, already unsealed.

He enters to retrieve it, and the door closes behind him.

The walls are entirely exposed reflective insulation, shiny but not bright, not brightening the mute black of the room. Something akin to confetti and not unlike the plastic over the faces of both the man in red and Harue, peeled off to expose nothing more horrible than their ordinary faces, albeit a brief moment before their suicides. I respond the way I always do when I see a small room, covered in tarps, camera on a tripod.

Our ghosts have leaked from their realm into ours through the internet, and once here—nothing, not at first. Each one we've seen has been in or from a Forbidden Room, sealed before there is a figure there at all. That is, they enter our world as energy, as essence, as subject, as emanation; they get stuck, blocked by our red tape. Then they coagulate, they take shape slowly, slowly come into focus; like cooking, like poplar seeds collecting at the corners of alleys. Reflective insulation can't reflect light, even if we expect it to—aluminum foil the worst mirror—but it bounces 96 percent of radiant energy, and I wonder if this makes a ghost manifest faster, come into focus more solidly. Something to do with electromagnetic waves and isotopes.

The walls are unimportant unless this material explains why the ghost in this room is different: This ghost speaks.

Forever, death was eternal loneliness.

The exact same sentiment Harue had expressed to Ryosuke before, in her apartment. Death is not an escape from the loneliness but rather is an extension of it, or at least that is what she feared: that our loneliness and isolation makes us despondent, turns us to ghosts, and so we are already dead inside our bodies.

Ryosuke tries to run.

Ryosuke's ghost in this warehouse Forbidden Room gives the same plea as all the rest:

Tasukete. Tasukete. Tasukete.

Ryosuke stops trying to escape, trying to run. *Don't ask me. What's that got to do with me.* He can't or refuses to help this blur that steps into the center of the room. What is our connection to—what would we *have to do*—with eternal loneliness.

You're not real.

As he turns around, he covers his face with his hands in case he is wrong, not wanting to encounter this ghost, believing, despite his exclamation, that he might. Just as Ryosuke's hands drop, we can see the black blur of the ghost appear again. In his horror, Ryosuke stumbles back and reveals the ghost to us, as if it were only visible when it is visible to him. As if the ghost needs to be triangulated by all our eyes, be seen seeing being seen. Contracted into being.

That Ryosuke *refuses to acknowledge death* in this moment seems to demonstrate his continued naivety and immaturity: This is not a confrontation with death. It's a confrontation with a ghost that exists despite death—a reckoning that our bodies can't contain us, and that death is inconsequential. Death has never been the trauma, nothing to do with us—abjection nothing to do with mortality, the corpse.

Ryosuke assumes that this ghost, like the one in the library, should *disappear* if he catches it—or if he proves it was never there to begin with. When he tries to catch it, he sprints across the room and his hands firmly plant on either shoulder of the ghost. Ryosuke's eyes move between the blurry hands and the face he's confronting and an impossibly tangible body. For several seconds, seeming an eternity of horror and understanding, he is still, silent, eyes fixed on the ghost, until he falls backward to the floor, perhaps trying to crawl away but stuck.

We and Ryosuke become *hybrid*, his eyes our own, looking up at the ghost standing over us, all in black with a white face, shadows for eyes.

I am real.

He moves toward us, two slow, footless steps before he becomes even less material, phases closer still and to the left. It's a threatening movement, like a predator, a cat adjusting line of sight, a bird calculating depth and distance. A slow, continuous motion that has nothing to do with the floor.

Then he glitches, with the sound of television static or connectivity, above and behind himself for a moment before returning, even closer. Proximity doesn't bring him into focus, and, despite his movement, light never changes how it plays on his face—skeletal, shadow eyes and jaw.

The sound of dial-up, connecting. Our eyes finally move to accommodate his height, and our sight pans as he drops to our level, our eye to this unseen, dark, blurry eye.

In the final seconds of the shot, before cutting to Ryosuke's reaction, the eyelashes, eyelid, and black empty eyes become unblurred, the first irruption out of a mediated death, a stark eerie contrast to the remaining blurry and anonymous flesh.

■

Portraiture is no longer a reflection or projection of our subjectivity. Bacon's, a parody: Their blurred moving faces cannot be contracted into a single form by our eyes. He demanded they be displayed behind glass, forcing us to bob our heads like birds to avoid any glare as we approach the art.

Our wholeness, as in the mirror, is only made possible by the gaze of the other. So these distorted, fractured, fragmented faces, unable to be understood properly, fail to become whole, subject.

So when we face them, there is no gaze, no eyes or face through which we are seen. And in these moments, we *also* fail to become whole, subject.

In a Bacon portrait, flesh is proven not only to be stretched taut over something that churns but also to be churning itself. Our flesh, our language, breaks and still nothing shows up to reassure us. We *abject* in the face of these—identity, an impossible matter.

■

I had lost any attraction to him long ago. Sexual desire was, what, specious, at best—controlled and taken and bartered with. I hid my undesire for a long time, and I was good at it. Years of forcing myself or pretending to cum for him without an ounce of pleasure in my body—organs, mechanical. A penis, hardly genital.

Of course he caught on, eventually, and it broke him, I think. *You can't even kiss me right anymore, probably because you are fucking those guys across the hallway every time I leave the apartment.* I kiss you plenty. *You do this*, and he demonstrated, childish kisses as my jaw locked and my lips pursed. *This is how you're supposed to fucking do it*, and he demonstrated. I was pinned to the bed, suddenly only half-dressed, saying so many variations of *no* that the snakes couldn't be kept from wedging themselves between my lips.

■

To become a subject, we have to individuate ourselves from our mothers who, when we are infants, are seemingly inextricable. Turning away from the nipple, when we feel sated, is that first time. That is, to become subject, we must first *ab-ject*.

K's theory is a version or amalgamation or synthesis of Freud's theories of disavowal, taboo, and ambivalence, all of which have to do with what we repress not only to protect ourselves but also form our selves.

It's all transitive property and math: K's maternal abjection is a process of repression. Experiencing abjection is a return of the repressed. We react the way we do because we fear, as Freud claims, falling back into the mother's body, becoming one with her again, becoming indistinct from, which is a fear of losing our subjectivity. Freud calls this fear and response the uncanny, *das Unheimliche.*

K says that enduring the abject is *a massive and sudden emergence of uncanniness.* These theories differ in only two ways: First, the repressed does not necessarily return while the abject is always threatening to. Second is severity—the same mechanism, but abjection is *more violent.*

■

I continue to purchase books by and about K, even now, having already tried to step away from this project I once considered to be over. There was the hundred-dollar, just-published, thick intellectual history I regret buying. Twice, I accidentally bought books I already owned (that inferiority complex convinced me I couldn't have already read it). The one that applies her theory to art, proven unusable (*unusable* because it was too dense to be understandable). Here next to me now is my most recent purchase, this, the Routledge *Julia Kristeva*, part of their Critical Thinkers series. It's a slim, cheap volume with a heathered sage cover barely featuring a person in profile from top of nose down to shoulders—just a sliver, just hardly there on the right of the image, the person beyond the page, out of focus and mostly out of sight.

It's a book that does not rely on K's face to sell. In fact, each book in the series features the same image in a different color: Deleuze is red, Žižek is fuchsia, Blanchot is brown, and Baudrillard, just a little lighter than K.

It is the *Chris Teva for Dummies* that I had originally searched for, asked for, went to my faculty for—to no avail. How could it have taken me so long to find this, the book that would have once helped me the most, then. How was it so buried under all the rest.

It seems this book is neither offered nor referenced in academia. Maybe because it is little known. Maybe because K is too sacred for there to be an alternative, an idol. And, indeed, maybe because *everyone knows Chris Teva*, and maybe because *not as many people know who this is as you think.*

It's the last book on K that I'm sitting with while writing this. I may still suffer a grave misunderstanding, but I have come to know several things.

Let me write them:

First, that a *Chris Teva for Dummies* is still challenging. While it does seem to effectively define abjection according to K's own writing rather than, say, Creed's, it still has all these sentences that require previous knowledge or exposure: *The genotext is the motility between words.* In something like a pull quote, designed to draw attention to the explicit definition: *When the subject severs the signifying import of semiotic affects, it becomes impossible for her to say something meaningful.* Elsewhere, defining *ego*: *Is it some kind of innate self, waiting to be cured or discovered? Or is it merely an effect of internal processes in relation with social forces?*

I literally do not know.

Second, that those who were meant to be able to help me could not. I recall how one faculty member pulled *PoH* from their shelf as I pulled my own copy from my backpack: not only my ability to flip directly to the passage we were discussing but also their lack of physical engagement with the text—those conspicuously unmarked pages beyond that first chapter. I also recall the criticism my work received: *Why not Althusser, whose primary theory is subjectivity.* I wish I could go back, now, and say, *Why not. Because your question is irrelevant. (Stop trying to make me like you.)*

Third, that academia, that academics, protect themselves from outsiders by building a space in which their knowledge can be sacred, a place far away from the folk and queerfolk; by altering the reality of that space so that they can never be wrong, never need to admit ignorance; and, once an intruder has demonstrated their loyalty, by converting and brainwashing them.

What I know is that I, *I*, had no value to them. (*I* still has none.) Instead, I was admitted for (and eventually succeeded because of) my overwhelming sense of inferiority and my glaring impostor syndrome, both of which made me susceptible to their power. I'd become accustomed to subjection. And subjugation.

■

He'd pull up a website and he'd scroll until we found the first video that was long enough and enjoyable (pleasurable) enough for both of us. This is not unlike how a previous ex and I would get off—mutually, parallel, over porn we shared with each other. It's clear to me now that, like most of what he did, this was a way to condition me, to gaslight me into something more extreme, more violent—something worse.

He started to encourage (challenge) me to make the choice myself—*it's hot*, he'd say, to know what I find sexy. He'd leer over it, over my supposedly leering over something else. Sexual because predatory, and predatory because violent.

This video: He'd like it because it has Rafael Alencar in it, but I won't like it because the bottom is too skinny (too like me). This video: Definitely down to watch two guys fucking after working out, but he would be made to feel more insecure about his own body. Although Rafael Alencar obviously spends more time in the gym than anyone in this video. This video: Do I choose it because I know he'll like it because I discovered, already, that he has seen it already, trusting that a knowledge of his desire will make his desire grow; or will that choice belie my discovery, making all this all the more violent. Oh, this one: because both of these guys are unlike me.

If I chose wrong, I had to comfort him. If I chose *so* wrong that he hit me, I had to comfort him.

If I chose right or wrong and he chose again—a part of me still feels his knuckles against my scalp, my hair in his hands (before he made me shave it off), holding my face up to the computer screen to watch, my mouth hanging open to imitate the pleasure I couldn't feel. His desire for control indistinguishable from his desire to control my desire. The rim, that absence.

■

What I know, now, is that my mother was never wrong (has never been). I know that K's theories are *not* universal:

PoH, especially, is keenly aware of cultural differences regarding taboo and cleansing rituals—that is, it admits its particularity. What is abject is subjective, but she suggests that the *process of* abjection is universal, human. Her theory is a theory of language, ultimately: Subjectivity refers to the signification of *I* (only ever *I* in English, and only ever *je* in her French), this solitary meaning standing against all non-meaning, against things that may collapse what *I/je* represents. Just a single word.

I don't know Japanese, but, ever the good otaku, I dig for difficult and abstruse information—my *currency*.

Japanese, like many other languages, I'm sure (I could check, but), does not have that single word under which we individuate ourselves from the amniotic *everything*. Japanese has ten: *atakushi*, *atashi*, *boku*, *jibun*, *ore*, *uchi*, *washi*, *ware*, *watakushi*, *watashi*. There are at least fifteen ways to say *you*. This does not seem like an obvious inside/outside, here/not-here, me/undoes-me. Too many letters, now, in the equation.

Or maybe we are quick to claim *not universal* only if we want to disprove a woman or discredit theory as an approach to anything, only if we are already prejudiced against her. Instead, perhaps we just need to squint: We come into our subjectivity *in stages*. From our mothers, once we have a conscious sense of (linguistic) gender, when we face an elderly man, once we can distinguish between formal and casual, military and humble, and so on, until we know who we are in relation to any other individual. See ourself seeing, meeting the gaze and the abject.

I've been squinting, and it is not clear to me how K's theory remains universal today. Developed over the span of well over a decade, four decades ago, K reintroduced material conditions, the body, into studies of language: Spatial comportment and a physical vessel are requirements of our subjectivity. And then, internet: The rules of embodiment and subjectivity *must* have changed since then—the limits of our bodies always expanding and contracting, our infinitude.

■

I could say that I did the sad ex thing, engaged in that kind of casual *stalking* we've all come to know—reading through all his vagueposts, the song lyrics, the pictures of new decorations in his new apartment, and seeing just how quickly he rebounded, the candlelit handholding, the location tagging for various dates, the carefully cropped images of gifts and flowers. Those who call it *stalking* are the same who claim we do it when we are bored, when we are lonely; we are sometimes just curious. But, of course, it is not *stalking* at all: There is no approach, no pursuit, and, from the other's perspective, no known attention to be unwanted, not if we withhold our tapping.

Private, public.

But this could only be true while his Facebook and Instagram profiles existed, before they were deleted; and I supplemented this information anyway.

I wasn't lonely, I was afraid; and the internet continued to be a tool for safety. Again, the digital can corroborate our perception and confirm our suspicions, albeit in all these imperfect and imprecise ways—never *real* or *true* but always real and true *enough*—and, again, I used Scruff to measure distance and, thus, safety.

■

But the internet knows a secret—the deeper part of the internet that I keep out of my search and browser histories but that my computer knows (and others could find) regardless: I saved his pictures. These Scruff, Chaturbate, OkCupid profile pictures of him, shirtless, shaved or unshaved, tempting and unreachable, these images of my violent ex made suddenly violenceless in front of all my conditional identities. Out of shame, I delete them; out of curiosity, perhaps fear, I return to them. I restore them from my deleted folder before deleting them again, keeping them out of sight but never entirely gone—always looming, very near, at the periphery.

I didn't recognize the power play, my participation, in some way, in the system he designed for our relationship: I shouldn't have been raped on cam, but I was. I shouldn't have these photos, but I do. My body wasn't mine to control; my sex, my desire weren't mine to control; but look, now, how he doesn't have it. Look at how vulnerable, that naked body. If I make it happen again at my desk, look at how easily his is now mine. If I know he is still *there*, then I know he is not *here*. I feel safer each time I check and find no new uploads anywhere, as if his presence could grow weaker, his emanation fade.

I check, occasionally, to see if the untagged pictures from our wedding (again, his drunken half-blink) have disappeared from social media's memory. They remain difficult to find, but they haven't vanished, not yet.

Sleuthing for these in friends' and family members' albums and uploads led me to a new index of him there: His mother is newly friends with this unknown thirty-something-year-old queer man from Chicago. His shoes and his hair are both mine. His favorite ice cream flavor, also mine. Our interests overlap; our cover photos, from the same movie.

We are *like*. I do—I feel an immediate and unquestionable kinship with him.

His photos, like mine, are not usually of himself: cake, bouquet, bouquet, pumpkin, two pumpkins, pumpkin seeds, cookies. There are others, of course, hidden behind the first or just less visible due to time: I notice a set of hands I know, hands I remember. A tattoo that I watched be tattooed. I've touched that jacket. There's a snake in an aquarium. His television-screen-shaped thumbnails.

Like a cuckoo, he has existed in someone else's profile—no need for his own. He's there, in eight months of photos, bent torso, back turned, reaching limbs. Not blurry or out of focus, but only ever implied out of frame. Never the subject.

■

I told my mother that this imaginary book began with a simple curiosity, *Can I find it*, but I never told her what I was looking for, always supplanted by other atrocities. Still, I haven't explained how this curiosity resulted in horror, a reckoning with the way everything on the internet is cataloged and indexed, referenced and duplicated, eternal—the way that nothing is real but always once was.

When I remember, when I recall him, when I conjure the abuse, my body responds in ways that I, *I*, do not. (*Show, don't tell.*) I am quiet and stiff-jawed, my whole body stiff now; my partner, behind me, on the couch, unaware of what these words on my computer screen say, unknowing what my language is made of. Unknowable, that it feels like he remains here, under my flesh, especially in those dark moments of inferiority or weakness or loneliness. Look, now, at my sudden dysphoria: I know I was not safe but think I am now, except for how my body still knows it isn't.

If we are to believe anything that K says, if there is only one point, only one thing to believe, it is that we are heterogeneous. And look at how appropriately my body responds: disgust/desire. My bodies, existing in parallel: the one *here* and the one *then*, which doesn't exist anymore and yet somehow—just does. Just everything after. And everything before.

BIBLIOGRAPHY

akidearest. "This Is Japan's Otaku Killer." *YouTube*, 26 Jan. 2021, https://www.youtube.com/watch?v=jQwAw_OCVaA.

Althusser, Louis. "Ideology and Ideological State Apparatus (Notes Towards an Investigation)." *Lenin and Philosophy and Other Essays*, edited by Ben Brewster, Monthly Review Press, 2001, pp. 85–126.

Ancuta, Katarzyna. "Ghosts and the Machines: Spectres of the Technological Revolution." *Asian Journal of Literature, Culture and Society*, vol. 2, 2008.

Arya, Rina. *Abjection and Representation: An Exploration of Abjection in the Visual Arts, Film and Literature*. Palgrave Macmillan, 2014.

Barrett, Estelle. *Kristeva Reframed*. I. B. Tauris, 2011.

Barthes, Roland. *Image-Music-Text*. Translated by Stephen Heath, Hill and Wang, 1977.

———. "Kristeva's *Semeiotike*." *The Rustle of Language*. Translated by Richard Howard, Hill and Wang, 1986, pp. 168–71.

Beardsworth, Sara G. *The Philosophy of Julia Kristeva*. Open Court, 2020.

bh_so. "Why Is Domo Used Also to Say Hello?" *Japanese Language Stack Exchange*, 12 Jan. 2016, https://japanese.stackexchange.com/questions/30346/why-is-domo-used-also-to-say-hello.

Blake, Linnie, and Xavier Aldana Reyes. *Digital Horror: Haunted Technologies, Network Panic and the Found Footage Phenomenon*. I. B. Tauris, 2015.

Blow, Charles M. "Tyre Nichols's Death Is America's Shame." *New York Times*, 27 Jan. 2023, https://www.nytimes.com/2023/01/27/opinion/tyre-nichols-video.html.

Bourseul, Vincent. "The 'Uncanny' and the Queer Experience." *Recherches en psychanalyse*, vol. 10, no. 2, 2010, pp. 242–50.

Brock, Peyton. "'Pulse': How Kiyoshi Kurosawa's Terrifying J-Horror Exemplifies Our Year of Isolation." *Collider*, 14 July 2021, https://collider.com/pulse-movie-why-its-scary/.

Brown, Steven T. *Tokyo Cyberpunk: Posthumanism in Japanese Visual Culture*. Palgrave Macmillan, 2010.

Bukatman, Scott. *Terminal Identity: The Virtual Subject in Postmodern Science Fiction*. Duke University Press, 1993.

Burgess, Katherine. "Video Shows Police Kicking, Pepper Spraying, Beating Tyre Nichols After Traffic Stop." *Memphis Commercial Appeal*, 27 Jan. 2023, https://www.commercialappeal.com/story/news/crime/2023/01/28/tyre-nichols-videos-released/69848091007/

Butler, Judith. "Arguing with the Real." *Bodies That Matter: On the Discursive Limits of Sex*, Routledge, 1993.

———. "Passing, Queering: Nella Larsen's Psychoanalytic Challenge." *Passing*, edited by Carla Kaplan, Norton, 2007, pp. 417–34.

Chong, Wooju. "The Fleeting Nature of Techno-Horror: *Kairo's* Failure to Appeal to Gen Z." *Inquiries Journal*, vol. 13, no. 3, 2021, http://www.inquiriesjournal.com/a?id=1883.

Downey, Adrian M. "Review of *At the Risk of Thinking: An Intellectual Biography of Julia Kristeva*." *Philosophical Inquiry in Education*, vol. 27, no. 2, 2020, pp. 201–206.

"*Figure with Meat*. Francis Bacon, 1954." *Art Institute of Chicago*, 2016, https://www.artic.edu/artworks/4884/figure-with-meat.

Fisk, Robert. "Why Do Television Producers Think a Grey Blob Over a Dead Person's Face Shows Respect?" *Independent*, 21 July 2014, https://www.independent.co.uk/voices/comment/why-do-television-producers-think-a-grey-blob-over-a-dead-person-s-face-shows-respect-9617402.html.

Fleischmann, T. *Time Is the Thing a Body Moves Through*. Coffee House Press, 2019.

Fournier, Lauren. *Autotheory as Feminist Practice in Art, Writing, and Culture*. MIT Press, 2021.

Freud, Sigmund. "Remembering, Repeating and Working-Through (Further Recommendations on the Technique of Psycho-Analysis)." 1914. *The Standard Edition of the Complete Psychological Works of Sigmund Freud, Vol. XII (1911–1913)*, Vintage, 2001, pp. 145–56.

Google. "Ranking Results—How Google Search Works." *Discover How Google Search Works*, www.google.com/search/howsearchworks/how-search-works/ranking-results/#relevance.

Grassmuck, Volker. "'I'm Alone, but Not Lonely': Japanese *Otaku*-Kids Colonize the Realm of Information and Media." Cornell Japanese Animation Society, 1990. *Wayback Machine*, https://web.archive.org/web/20120113075055/http://www.cjas.org/~leng/otaku-e.htm.

Gross, Elizabeth. "The Body of Signification." *Abjection, Melancholia, and Love: The Work of Julia Kristeva*, edited by John Fletcher and Andrew Benjamin, Routledge, 1990, pp. 80–123.

Hey, Daniel Stephen. *The Malady Lingers On: The Abject and Contemporary Asian Horror Cinema*. 2018. University of Salford, PhD dissertation.

Hudson, Seán. "A Queer Aesthetic: Identity in Kurosawa Kiyoshi's Horror Films." *Film-Philosophy*, vol. 22, no. 3, Sept. 2018, pp. 448–464.

Hughes, Kit. "Ailing Screens, Viral Video: Cinema's Digital Ghosts in Kiyoshi Kurosawa's *Pulse*." *Film Criticism*, vol. 36, no. 2, 2011, pp. 22–42.

Jones, Steve. "The Technologies of Isolation: Apocalypse and Self in Kurosawa Kiyoshi's *Kairo*." *Japanese Studies*, vol. 30, no.2, Sept. 2010.

Kairo. Dir. Kiyoshi Kurosawa. Toho Company, 2001.

Keane, Tim. "The Unsparing Pages of Francis Bacon." *Hyperallergic*, 28 Dec. 2019, https://hyperallergic.com/534981/the-unsparing-pages-of-francis-bacon/.

Kerekes, David and David Slater. *Killing for Culture: From Edison to ISIS*. Headpress, 2016.

Koestenbaum, Wayne. *Humiliation*. Picador, 2011.

Kristeva, Julia. *Desire in Language: A Semiotic Approach to Literature and Art*. Edited by Leon S. Roudiez, Columbia University Press, 1980.

———. "On Julia Kristeva's Couch." Chicago Humanities Festival, 19 Oct. 2013, https://www.youtube.com/watch?v=b-AzikJn_uc.

———. *Powers of Horror: An Essay on Abjection*. Translated by Leon S. Roudiez, Columbia University Press, 1982.

———. "*Revolution in Poetic Language*." *The Kristeva Reader*, edited by Toril Moi, Blackwell Publishing, 1986, pp. 89–136.

———. *The Severed Head: Capital Visions*. Translated by Jody Gladding, Columbia University Press, 2014.

Kunkle, Sheila. "Psychosis in a Cyberspace Age." *Other Voices*, vol. 1, no. 3, Jan. 1999, http://www.othervoices.org/1.3/skunkle/psychosis.php.

Kusina, Jeanne Marie. "Difference, Repetition, Disappearance, and Death: A Deleuzian Consideration of Kiyoshi Kurosawa's *Kairo*." *Rhizomes*, vol. 16, Summer 2008.

Larson, Frances. "Why Public Beheading Videos Get Millions of Views." *TED*, June 2015, https://www.ted.com/talks/frances_larson_why_public_beheadings_get_millions_of_views.

Lelik, Timea Andrea. "Blurred Boundaries: Francis Bacon's Portraits." *World Literature Studies*, vol. 11, no. 4, 2019, pp. 84–96.

Lovasz, Adam. "'Would You Like to Meet a Ghost?': Repetition and Spectral Posthumanism in Kiyoshi Kurosawa's *Kairo*." *Horror Studies*, vol. 9, no. 2, 2018, pp. 249–63.

McAfee, Noëlle. *Julia Kristeva*. Routledge, 2004.

McGowan, Todd. *The Real Gaze: Film Theory After Lacan*. State University of New York Press, 2007.

McGrath, Thomas. "The Secret Story of How They Caught Canada's Cannibal Pornstar Killer." *DangerousMinds*, 31 July 2012, https://dangerousminds.net/comments/exclusive_the_secret_story_of_how_they_caught_canadas_cannibal_pornstar.

McRoy, Jay. *Nightmare Japan*. Brill, 2008.

Nelson, Maggie. *The Art of Cruelty: A Reckoning*. W. W. Norton, 2012.

Phillips, Robert. "Abjection." *TSQ*, 1 May 2014, pp. 1–2, https://read.dukeupress.edu/tsq/article/1/1-2/19/91761/Abjection.

Rankine, Claudia. *Citizen*. Greywolf Press, 2014.

Ribeiro, Paulo Victor. "TikTok Livestreamed a User's Suicide—Then Got Its PR Strategy in Place Before Calling the Police." *The Intercept*, 6 Feb. 2020, https://theintercept.com/2020/02/06/tiktok-suicide-brazil/.

Rombe, Nicholas. "Julia Kristeva's Face." *The Rumpus*, 14 June 2011, https://therumpus.net/2011/06/14/julia-kristevas-face/.

Ryle, Gilbert. "Descartes' Myth." *The Concept of Mind*. 1949. Department Filosofie en Religiewetenschap, Universiteit Utrecht, https://www.phil.uu.nl/~joel/3027/GilbertRyleDescartesMyth.pdf.

Schmitz, Bettina, and Julia Jansen. "Homelessness or Symbolic Castration? Subjectivity, Language Acquisition, and Sociality in Julia Kristeva and Jacques Lacan." *Hypatia*, vol. 20, no. 2, 2005, pp. 69–87.

Schuh, Becca. "A Blueprint for an Anticapitalist Life." *The Nation*, 4 Sept. 2019, https://www.thenation.com/article/archive/time-is-the-thing-a-body-moves-through-t-fleischmann-book-review/.

Sconce, Jeffery. *Haunted Media: Electronic Presence from Telegraphy to Television*. Duke University Press, 2000.

Shapero, Julia. "Nichols Footage: Treated Like a 'Premiere of a Movie.'" *The Hill*, 27 Jan. 2023, https://thehill.com/homenews/state-watch/3834083-eric-garners-daughter-criticizes-release-of-tyre-nichols-footage-treated-like-a-premiere-of-a-movie/.

Sycamore, Mattilda Bernstein. *The Freezer Door*. Semiotext(e), 2020.

Trumbore, Dave. "'The Blair Witch Project' Effect: How Found Footage Shaped a Generation of Filmmaking." *Collider*, 16 Sept. 2016, https://collider.com/blair-witch-found-footage-movies/#sequel.

Tufekci, Zeynep. "We're Building a Dystopia Just to Make People Click on Ads." *TED*, 17 Nov. 2017, https://www.youtube.com/watch?v=iFTWM7HV2UI.

Tunheim Partners. "The Blair Web Project: The E-Marketing of a Movie." *E-Strategy*, 2009. *Wayback Machine*, https://web.archive.org/web/20090614075546/http://e-strategy.com/internetmarketingarticle.asp?section=Reports&story=online-movie-marketing-blair-witch-project.

Wetmore, Kevin J., Jr. *Post-9/11 Horror in American Cinema*. Continuum, 2012.

———. "Technoghosts and Culture Shocks: Sociocultural Shifts in American Remakes of J-Horror." *Post Script*, vol. 28, Winter–Spring 2009, pp. 72–81.

White, Jerry. *The Films of Kiyoshi Kurosawa: Master of Fear*. Stone Bridge Press, 2007.

Whitney, Brian, and Anna Yourkin. *My Son, The Killer: The Untold Story of Luka Magnotta and "1 Lunatic 1 Ice Pick."* Wildblue Press, 2018.

Wilden, Anthony. *The Language of the Self: "The Function of Language in Psychoanalysis," by Jacques Lacan*. Johns Hopkins University Press, 1968.

Zeki, Semir, and Tomohiro Ishizu. "The 'Visual Shock' of Francis Bacon: An Essay in Neuroesthetics." *Frontiers in Human Neuroscience*, vol. 7, Dec. 2013, pp. 1–15.

CRUX, THE GEORGIA SERIES IN LITERARY NONFICTION

Debra Monroe, *My Unsentimental Education*
Sonja Livingston, *Ladies Night at the Dreamland*
Jericho Parms, *Lost Wax: Essays*
Priscilla Long, *Fire and Stone: Where Do We Come From? What Are We? Where Are We Going?*
Sarah Gorham, *Alpine Apprentice*
Tracy Daugherty, *Let Us Build Us a City*
Brian Doyle, *Hoop: A Basketball Life in Ninety-Five Essays*
Michael Martone, *Brooding: Arias, Choruses, Lullabies, Follies, Dirges, and a Duet*
Andrew Menard, *Learning from Thoreau*
Dustin Parsons, *Exploded View: Essays on Fatherhood, with Diagrams*
Clinton Crockett Peters, *Pandora's Garden: Kudzu, Cockroaches, and Other Misfits of Ecology*
André Joseph Gallant, *A High Low Tide: The Revival of a Southern Oyster*
Justin Gardiner, *Beneath the Shadow: Legacy and Longing in the Antarctic*
Emily Arnason Casey, *Made Holy: Essays*
Sejal Shah, *This Is One Way to Dance: Essays*
Lee Gutkind, *My Last Eight Thousand Days: An American Male in His Seventies*
Cecile Pineda, *Entry without Inspection: A Writer's Life in El Norte*
Anjali Enjeti, *Southbound: Essays on Identity, Inheritance, and Social Change*
Clinton Crockett Peters, *Mountain Madness: Found and Lost in the Peaks of America and Japan*
Steve Majors, *High Yella: A Modern Family Memoir*
Julia Ridley Smith, *The Sum of Trifles*
Siân Griffiths, *The Sum of Her Parts: Essays*
Ned Stuckey-French, *One by One, the Stars: Essays*
John Griswold, *The Age of Clear Profit: Collected Essays on Home and the Narrow Road*
Debra Monroe, *It Takes a Worried Woman: Essays*
Joseph Geha, *Kitchen Arabic: How My Family Came to America and the Recipes We Brought with Us*
Lawrence Lenhart, *Backvalley Ferrets: A Rewilding of the Colorado Plateau*
Sarah Beth Childers, *Prodigals: A Sister's Memoir of Appalachia*

Jodi Varon, *Your Eyes Will Be My Window: Essays*
Sandra Gail Lambert, *My Withered Legs and Other Essays*
Brooke Champagne, *Nola Face: Memoirs of a Truth-Telling Latina in the Big Easy*
Maddie Norris, *The Wet Wound: An Elegy in Essays*
Cris Mazza, *The Decade of Letting Things Go: A Postmenopause Memoir*
Lydia Paar, *The Exit Is the Entrance: Essays on Escape*
Joe Bonomo, *Play This Book Loud: Noisy Essays*
Wes Jamison, *My Corpse Inside*

A provocative and meticulously structured exploration of identity, language, and the body, *My Corpse Inside* exposes the thin and increasingly blurry line between the physical and the digital, between the living and the dead. Wes Jamison contends with the complex and disturbing relationship of sexuality and violence through a torrent of virtual horrors—shock sites, hookup apps, beheading videos, and creepshots—as well as through Jamison's own experiences of being surveilled and exploited online. Inspired by Kiyoshi Kurosawa's master horror film *Kairo*, which portrays ghosts overflowing into our reality through the internet, this fragmented book-length essay clarifies Julia Kristeva's infamously esoteric theory of abjection and subjectivity and updates it for today's constant virtuality. *My Corpse Inside* is a disquieting work that asks readers to confront the violence, fetish, horror, and loneliness inherent in our eternal connectivity.

"*My Corpse Inside* reads like a two-hundred-page slingshot, whipping from Kristeva to Angelspit, 2 Girls 1 Cup to Althusser, Michael Brown to Japanese Technohorror, all the while nakedly processing the author's own abuse. Ultimately, Jamison explores the body, the disembodied, the other-bodied, and our delicate agency that laces them. This book is more dexterous than anything I've read in years. How queer, indeed."—**MIAH JEFFRA**, author of *The Violence Almanac*

"Jamison has woven a fascinating, troubling, utterly revealing text of our contemporary landscape of screens, erotics, power, and violence."—**MARCO WILKINSON**, author of *Madder: A Memoir in Weeds*

"Sharply intelligent and deeply compassionate, *My Corpse Inside* compels us to look at what we often turn away from: the complexities of the body and language, sex and violence, death and belonging. Here is a mind that's wide open, an intellect that pulls us in, a gaze that won't be put off but keeps searching—relentlessly, brilliantly, acutely—for answers."—**RANDON BILLINGS NOBLE**, author of *A Harp in the Stars* and *Be with Me Always*

WES JAMISON is an assistant professor of English at Defiance College. They were awarded the 2021 Quill Prose Award for their essay collection *Carrion*, and their essay *and Melancholia* was selected as a winner of Essay Press's Chapbook Contest. Their work has been nominated for the Pushcart Prize and selected as Notables in *Best American Essays*. Their work also appears in *DIAGRAM*, *The Rumpus*, *Tupelo Quarterly*, *After the Art*, and elsewhere. Jamison currently lives in the Midwest with their partner and cat.

Cover design: Erin Kirk Cover photo: Adobe Stock / DRasa Author photo: Mitchell Boudoin

THE UNIVERSITY OF GEORGIA PRESS
ATHENS, GEORGIA 30602 WWW.UGAPRESS.ORG